How to Buy Insurance and Save Money

How to Buy Insurance and Save Money

Joseph Newman — Directing Editor

U.S.NEWS & WORLD REPORT BOOKS

A division of U.S.News & World Report, Inc.

WASHINGTON, D.C.

Contents

Illustrations

Acknowledgments

The editors have had the assistance of a number of insurance experts in gathering and in checking the material for this book. They are indebted especially to Philip Gordis, lecturer on insurance at the Bernard M. Baruch College of the City University of New York, for his major contribution to the researching and writing of the manuscript. Valuable assistance was also received from the Health Insurance Institute, Institute of Life Insurance, Insurance Information Institute, Martin L. Kamerow, C.P.A., Riggs National Bank, and the Social Security Administration. Roslyn Grant edited the manuscript and coordinated the editorial work on the book.

PART ONE

Your
Life
Insurance

CHAPTER 1

Why
Life
Insurance

With apologies to Alexander Pope, we begin this book by saying that the proper study of insurance is insurance. This, unfortunately, is not understood by many people who buy life insurance.

One of the reasons there is so much confusion about life insurance, with money often being foolishly wasted and families being inadequately protected, is that the subject is mixed up with matters not truly related to insurance.

The phrase "life insurance" itself is somewhat misleading. It implies "insuring one's life." But man has yet to discover how to insure his life so that it might be continued forever and guaranteed against death.

Instead of "life insurance," we might come closer to our meaning by using the phrase "death insurance" because the policy we buy is intended to insure our beneficiaries against the economic consequences resulting from premature death.

Life insurance can be and is being made to serve purposes other than insurance—such as creating a savings or investment fund. We will later take up the function of life insurance in building a savings fund to be used for such purposes as the education of children and retirement. But the focus of our treatment is on the subject of insurance—not savings or investment.

Creating an "instant estate"

Life insurance is an extraordinary device which enables you, should you die, to provide for your dependents with a sizable amount of money you do not possess while you are alive. How explain this miracle—the creation of an "instant estate" in favor of your dependents when you do not possess such an estate while alive?

The magic, we might say, is in the numbers. Life insurance is a game of numbers and a game of fate. It may be written in heaven, but on earth we know not who will live and who will die in any given year. Nevertheless, the genius of man is such that he has discovered an amazing phenomenon—of each thousand boys and girls who are born in a given year, a certain number will die. Of those who survive the first year, a number will die in their second year. Of those who survive the second year, a number will die in their third year; and so on until, perhaps around one hundred years after the birth of this group of 1,000 boys and girls, the last survivor will have died.

Our men of science may not be able to identify beforehand the individuals who will be struck down in a given year, but they *have* been able to discover a law of averages which gives us quite an accurate forecast of the number who will die within a given age group in a given year. The magic of life insurance derives from this law of averages.

This ability to forecast the number who will die within a given age group in a given year makes it possible for us to calculate how much each of us must contribute each year to provide a sum of money for the families of those who will not survive. For example, if the law of averages says that two of our class of 1,000 men and women will not sur-

The U.S. Death Rate Per 1,000 Persons
1900-1974

Year	Rate	Year	Rate
1900	17.2	1940	10.8
1905	15.9	1945	10.6
1910	14.7	1950	9.6
1915	13.2	1955	9.3
1920	13.0	1960	9.5
1925	11.7	1965	9.4
1930	11.3	1970	9.5
1935	10.9	1974	9.2

During the first half of this century there was a sharp drop in the death rate in the United States, but there has been relatively little change since mid-century. Recent studies suggest, however, an increase in male mortality, particularly at younger ages. The trend in female mortality is less clear, with different patterns based on age and race emerging.

Source: National Center for Health Statistics

vive this year, each of us could contribute $20 toward a pool of $20,000 which would provide $10,000 to each of the two unlucky families.

By sharing the cost of the benefit payment (known as "death benefit"), the entire class, including those marked for death later in the year, in effect makes a contribution to the families of the two unfortunate men. The contribution is not an expression of concern or sympathy for the mourning families. In fact, the contributors do not even know the other members in their insured class and so do not know who are the recipients of their money.

They make their contributions as a matter of self-interest. They have no way of knowing but that *they* may be the next ones marked to go. If we all knew not only how many were going to die but also who they were, those who knew they would survive year after year might not be disposed to make a contribution to the families of those who were disappearing year after year.

Thus the game of life insurance is played with two elements—one that is known (the *number* who will die) and one that is not known (the *identity* of those who will die).

The entire class of a given age group undertakes to share the cost of supporting the families of the few who will die in a given year because no one in the class knows the great secret of whether he or she may next be marked for death. And by pooling their money, thousands of persons in a given age group can produce the magic of an "instant estate" and make a gift of many thousands of dollars to each of the families of their fallen classmates, at a relatively small annual cost to each contributor. The pooling of their money and the sharing of the cost of carrying the unfortunate families form a fundamental aspect of the extraordinary phenomenon we call insurance.

Why premiums increase

The amount we contribute each year so that we might be entitled to participate in this game (that is, so that our family might win the "prize money" should we die) is called an insurance "premium." That is the amount we must regularly pay to the insurance company which manages the game for us. Since more of us die each year we grow older, the number of claims for death benefits increases, and we must make greater contributions in the form of higher premiums to meet these claims. Thus the cost of life insurance must increase each year as we grow older. You can pay a fixed amount, if you prefer, but that would simply represent an averaging out of the increasing cost of life insurance over a given number of years. Thus, instead of contributing $20 as the amount due from you in the example used earlier, you might pay $40 so that in later years, when your insurance bill may have increased to $60, you can continue paying $40 because you had acquired a $20 credit through an earlier overpayment.

There can be no true "level-payment premium" simply because the mortality table, based on the facts of life and death, rules that members of a given age group must produce more money each year as more die and more dependents become eligible for death benefits. However, you can, as mentioned, strike an average of the annually rising costs over a given period of time and secure the appearance of a constant or "level" cost of insurance by making overpayments in the earlier years of your policy. These overpayments serve as credits to compensate for underpayments in later years, when the true cost of your insurance has gone above the average of "level" payment which has been arranged.

There is a counterpart to this form of "constant" or "level" premium payments. Instead of making any overpayments to meet the subsequent annual increase in the cost of your insurance, you may choose to continue paying the original price at which you entered the insurance pool. However, since the price increases each year in step with the increase in mortality and since you prefer to pay no more each year than you did in your first year, your share in the pool must decrease and your beneficiaries must accept smaller death benefits. This decreasing face value of your insurance while maintaining your premiums at the original cost level is another recognition of the fact that the true cost of insurance inevitably increases year after year. We can meet the increasing cost either by paying more money or taking less insurance protection.

Insurance combined with savings

If life insurance were limited strictly to insurance, these elementary principles would make it quite easy for us to understand what it is about. It would be as simple to understand as a lottery—each ticket entitles you (or your dependents) to a share of the pool composed of the sum of all the money gathered from the sale of all the tickets. You could buy as many tickets as you desire, so that your share in the pool would be greater or smaller in accordance with the amount you contributed to it. The money in the case of a lottery as in the case of insurance goes to the one (or his heirs) whose number is called.

But life insurance is not limited to insurance. Companies which engage in the business of insurance combine insurance with the equivalent of savings. And this has given rise to so many complications and such confusion that many buyers of life insurance are not altogether clear as to just what it is they are buying.

Policies which provide "pure" insurance are known as "term" because they are sold for specific terms—one year, five years, or longer. For a given amount of money (the premium), the term policy will protect your dependents against the economic consequences of your death. Should you die during the term the policy is in force, your beneficiaries will be paid the face amount of the policy. Should you still be alive when the term expires, the policy is dissolved, you no longer hold any interest in it, and the contract setting forth the provisions of the policy becomes a worthless scrap of paper which can be assigned to the wastebasket. Like a fire insurance policy, term pays in event of disaster. Otherwise it pays nothing. In the latter case, your premiums would have served simply to provide protection over a given period against an event which fortunately did not occur.

Types of term insurance

Term insurance takes various forms, the principal ones being the following:

• *Level renewable term.* This is the most common type of term insurance. The face value of the policy is fixed ("level"), and the premium increases with each successive period that the insurance is renewed (to meet the increasing cost of increasing mortality, as mentioned earlier). Policies are issued for different periods, usually one or five years, known as "one-year term" and "five-year term." Term, as a rule, is issued only to age sixty-five. Being "pure" insurance, without a cash-value savings fund to sustain it, term becomes extremely expensive at older ages, and relatively few policies of this kind are issued after age sixty-five. However, it is usually possible to convert the term policy, prior to its expiration, to cash-value insurance at a higher premium, of course.

• *Level nonrenewable term.* As in the preceding type, the death benefit is fixed. The premium also is constant, having been averaged out over the term period of five years or more. Unlike the preceding type, this policy cannot be renewed but it, too, can be converted to cash-value insurance at a higher premium before age sixty-five or seventy.

• *Decreasing term.* In this case, the premium is constant, and the death benefit decreases regularly during the term of the policy, usually varying between ten and twenty-five years. This type of insurance often is used to cover the outstanding amount due on the mortgage of a house. As the size of the mortgage decreases each year with each repayment of capital, so does the amount of insurance protection. Should a death occur in the course of the term, the death benefit would correspond roughly to the outstanding amount due on the mortgage, which could then be paid off so that the family of a fallen breadwinner could have their home free of indebtedness.

"Cash-value" insurance

If you take "pure" insurance and add a savings account to it, you produce what is known as "cash-value" insurance. Each premium payment, in effect, is divided into two parts. One pays for the insurance coverage (the counterpart of term) ; the other goes into "cash values" (the counterpart of a savings account). As the cash reserves increase with each annual payment, the amount of insurance coverage decreases. If the insurance company is called upon to pay a death benefit, it uses the cash values in the policy toward payment of the face amount which is due. In other words, the amount of insurance coverage at any given time is the face value less the savings which have accumulated in the policy with payments in excess of what would be required for "pure" term insurance.

For example, if the owner of a $10,000 cash-value policy dies at age sixty-five, after maintaining the policy for forty years, the savings in the policy would be $6,000 and the amount of insurance coverage would be $4,000, provided from the common pool established by members of the same age group, as explained earlier. The insurance company combines these two amounts from these two accounts when it pays the $10,000 death benefit.

Prior to his death, if he chose to do so, he could have borrowed money against the cash values in his policy, which would have served as collateral for the loan, usually made at interest rates of 5 percent or 6 percent annually. However, upon his death, the amount of the loan would have been deducted from the $10,000 death benefit payment envisaged as the original face value of the policy. Or the policyholder, instead of borrowing, could have "cashed in" the policy by withdrawing the $6,000 of accumulated savings. In that event, the policy would have been liquidated and the former owner would have lost the $4,000 of insurance coverage it had contained.

In other words, if you die without having borrowed any of the savings in your policy, your heirs receive the full face value amount of your insurance. If you live and borrow against the accumulated savings, the death benefit your heirs will receive is reduced by the amount you have borrowed. And if you decide to remove all your savings, then you lose your insurance policy altogether. The policyholder, therefore, has several options open to him which must be exercised very carefully.

The unusual and complicated aspect of cash-value insurance is the inseparable attachment of the cash reserves in the policy to the insurance coverage provided by the policy. Unlike an account in a bank, you can get at the savings you have accumulated in your insurance policy only by borrowing your own money and paying interest to the insurance company for the privilege. If you insist on getting your cash reserves without borrowing them, then you must give up the policy entirely, together with its remaining insurance coverage.

If the owner should live to age 100, when his policy will mature, the cash value of his policy would then equal the face value and there would be no insurance protection left in the policy at all. The centenarian would receive his cash savings, and the policy would be terminated.

Types of cash-value policies

There are many types of cash-value policies, varying with the size of the savings fund the policyholder desires to establish. The major types are the following:

• *Ordinary life,* also known as *whole life, straight life,*

Cash Values of Life Insurance

Approximate cash values per $1,000 of insurance for each of four types of
life insurance policies taken out at age 18.

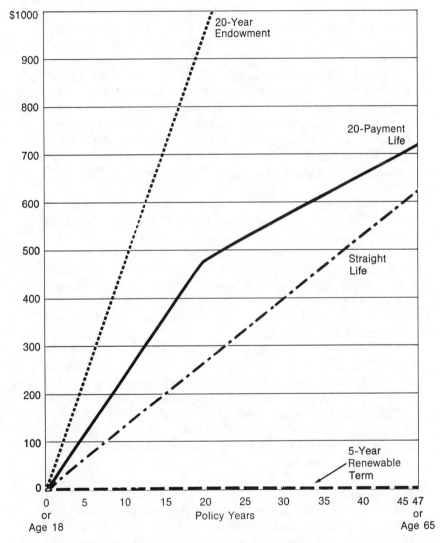

Source: Institute of Life Insurance

and *permanent life*. As some of the names imply, the policy-holder has insurance coverage for his beneficiaries as long as he lives, and he must continue paying premiums through-out his life. At the same time, in addition to insurance cov-erage, his policy is accumulating "cash values," or savings, as mentioned earlier. This is the most widely sold type of cash-value insurance.

• *Limited-payment insurance*. This is an intensified form of ordinary life insurance. Instead of annual premium pay-ments of lower amounts stretched out over an entire life-time, greater payments are packed into a limited number of years, often twenty years. After the final annual install-ment, the policy is "fully paid up," and insurance coverage is provided for the rest of your life without further pay-ments.

• *Endowment insurance*. This is a still more intensified form of life insurance, with the annual premiums being so high that the emphasis in the policy is on accumulating sav-ings. After a fixed number of years, again usually twenty, the policyowner can reap his "endowment"—the cash fund he originally set out to establish, possibly to meet the cost of a child's college education or some retirement aim. Should he die before the target date, his beneficiary would be paid the face value of the policy.

• *Variable life insurance*. This is a type of contract in which the premiums remain level but the benefits vary to reflect the gains and losses of funds invested in securities by the life insurance company. Designed as a hedge against inflation, the plan is predicated on the theory that the prices of securities rise during an inflationary era, and that death benefits paid out of the invested funds would increase as the prices of securities increase.

Term vs. cash-value

The two different kinds of insurance, term and cash-value, reflecting two rival schools of thought about life insurance, gave rise to heated debate inside and outside the insurance industry. The debate, starting more than forty years ago, continues to this day.

It is quite apparent that the industry can profit more

Purchases of Ordinary Life Insurance
("Average" Amounts, 1945-1975)

Americans with annual incomes under $7,500 purchased 27 percent of the new ordinary life policies on adults in 1974; persons with incomes between $7,500 and $9,999 purchased 22 percent; those with incomes ranging from $10,000 to $24,999 purchased 45 percent; and purchasers with incomes of $25,000 or more accounted for the remaining 6 percent. Nearly one out of three of all the new ordinary policies was purchased by persons between the ages of 15 and 24 in 1974, and over a quarter of all new ordinary policies were purchased by persons between the ages of 25 and 34.

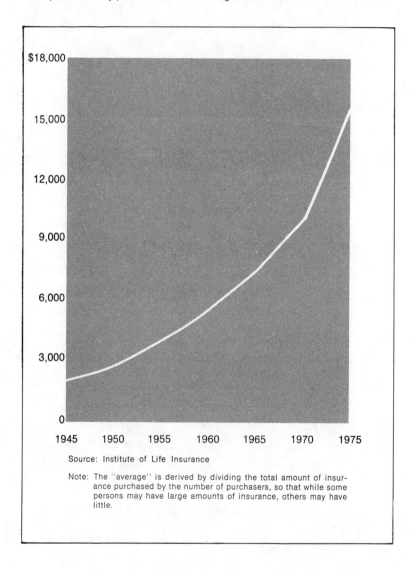

Source: Institute of Life Insurance

Note: The "average" is derived by dividing the total amount of insurance purchased by the number of purchasers, so that while some persons may have large amounts of insurance, others may have little.

Growth of Ordinary Life Insurance
In United States

(000,000 omitted)

Year	No. of Policies	Amount
1900	3	$ 6,124
1905	5	9,585
1910	6	11,783
1915	9	16,650
1920	16	32,018
1925	23	52,892
1930	32	78,576
1935	33	70,684
1940	37	79,346
1945	48	101,550
1950	64	149,116
1955	80	216,812
1960	95	341,881
1961	97	366,141
1962	99	391,048
1963	102	420,808
1964	104	457,868
1965	107	499,638
1966	109	541,022
1967	113	584,570
1968	116	633,392
1969	118	682,453
1970	120	734,730
1971	123	792,318
1972	126	853,911
1973	128	928,192
1974	131	1,009,038
1975	134	1,083,421

Note: Data include individual credit life insurance on loans of more than 10 years' duration.

Sources: *Spectator Year Book*, Institute of Life Insurance

from cash-value insurance than from term insurance by virtue of the fact that the former makes the accumulation of large sums of savings available to the insurance company for profitable investment. These savings, in effect, enable insurance companies to go beyond the strict area of insurance and into the field of investment.

That is not an argument against those companies which prefer to work with higher-cost cash-value insurance than with lower-cost term insurance. On the contrary, the argument might be advanced that the greater profits made through cash-value insurance enable the companies, if they choose, to pass on some of the benefits of these profits to their policyholders in the form of lower premium rates and improved terms of the policy.

Obviously there are strong points to be made on behalf of both types of insurance and a good case can be made for one or the other, depending on the financial strength, the objectives, and the personal circumstances of the individual involved. Our purpose is not to enter the debate between the two schools of thought but rather to assist the reader through the complicated and confusing world of insurance so that he might make a wise choice in selecting his coverage.

In that respect, it might be emphasized that the reader himself must make the decision because the insurance salesman with whom he must deal is an interested party, and the interests of the salesman may or may not serve those of the insurance buyer. The salesman of insurance, like the salesman in any store, has a variety of products he can deliver. He can usually earn a far greater commission (perhaps three or four times as much) from the sale of a given amount of cash-value insurance than from the sale of the same amount of term insurance. It is only human to expect him to be pushing cash-value insurance, as those we interviewed during the preparation of this book admitted they do.

Again, the interest of the salesman in pressing for a cash-value sale does not necessarily rule out cash-value as the kind which would best suit the customer's purpose. It simply means that the customer, discounting the special interest of the salesman, should be in a position to evaluate the merits of both types of insurance and then call on the salesman to de-

How Life Insurance Companies Invest Their Assets

1975

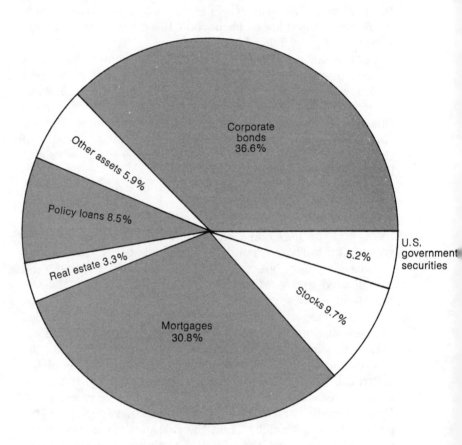

Corporate bonds 36.6%

Other assets 5.9%

Policy loans 8.5%

Real estate 3.3%

Mortgages 30.8%

Stocks 9.7%

5.2% U.S. government securities

Source: Institute of Life Insurance

liver the kind that he, the customer, thinks is best for the particular case at hand.

After all, it is you and your family who are most directly affected by your decision. And in insurance, as in many other fields of paramount importance, the individual directly concerned, rather than the salesman or the counselor, should be the one to make the final decision. This and subsequent chapters, going beyond the cursory review of the field of insurance in an earlier volume of this series, may help you toward that decision.

CHAPTER 2

Who Should Be Insured and How Much

Large sums of money are being wasted every year by purchases of insurance on the lives of persons who have no great need to be insured. Many fathers, for example, have allowed themselves to be persuaded to buy insurance policies on the lives of their school children. The argument often used is that purchase of a cash-value policy on the life of a child will enable him to hold the policy at a low-cost level throughout his life. Another point often made is that such a purchase will create a savings fund which would be available later to help meet the cost of the child's college education.

It is certainly true that a cash-value policy can be purchased at an early age at a lower cost per thousand dollars of insurance coverage than at an older age. And it is also true that, for those who cannot discipline themselves to save in a more profitable way, a cash-value policy accumulates savings which would be most welcome to meet the constantly soaring cost of higher education.

However, as indicated in the preceding chapter, the suggestion that anyone can beat the mortality table and get a better bargain by buying insurance at an earlier age is deceptive. The price of insurance is lower at a lower age because the risk of death (and your chances of collecting a death benefit) is lower. If the premium cost remains level and relatively low in subsequent years, that can be attributed to the fact that the savings element in the policy has been growing all the time and has been replacing the continuously shrinking element of insurance coverage. Though the face value of the policy remains constant, the shrinking amount of insurance coverage, as explained in Chapter 1, reflects increasing cost as the insured person grows older, and it is only the addition of the regularly increasing savings account to the diminishing insurance coverage which makes it possible to secure a level premium cost and a level death benefit.

The question of insuring children

The matter of insurance as an instrument of savings will be considered later. At this point we need only raise the question as to whether a child is the proper object of insurance, granted the fact that the cash outlay in premiums would be less than it would be if the policy were purchased later in life and the fact that the policy would become a vehicle for accumulating savings.

The answer might well be related to the purpose of insurance set forth at the beginning of this book. If the real and fundamental purpose is to provide dependents with insurance against the economic consequences of the untimely death of a breadwinner, then we must recognize that insurance on a child, who will continue living, will contribute not a penny toward the maintenance of a family which has lost its primary source of income. On the contrary, we might say that the burden of continuing to pay premiums for a child's policy may become greater or even impossible to carry following the death of a father.

Even more important is the fact that expenditure of money on a child's life insurance may divert money which might better have been invested in greater insurance on the life of the breadwinner. In the case of families which are inadequately protected by life insurance—and this is true of the majority of families in the United States—expenditure on a child's insurance at the expense of greater protection for the family through more insurance on the life of the breadwinner may be considered to be poor management of family finances.

Insurance for wives

A similar conclusion, with some qualification, might be made regarding insurance on the life of a wife. If the wife is working and contributing to the maintenance of the family, then the amount of her contribution or part of it might well be guaranteed by insurance on her life. If she is not employed outside the home, then some coverage often is recommended to help meet the cost of domestic services in event of her death. With the exception of a relatively small amount of coverage for such a contingency, insurance on the life of a wife, as in the case of that on the life of a child, could be a wasteful and dangerous diversion from the maximum possible amount of insurance at the point where it is needed—on the life of the family breadwinner.

If there is any doubt as to the extent to which most American families are underinsured, notwithstanding the impressive statistic that we have nearly $2 trillion of life insurance coverage in the United States, we need only recall the findings of *The Widows Study,* published in 1970 by the Life Insurance Management Association. They show that more than half the widows whose husbands died before age sixty-five received less than $5,000 in insurance benefits, and only 8 percent of them received as much as $25,000.

According to published estimates, the "average" American family is covered by over $26,000 of life insurance. This would meet the cost of funeral and related death expenses, and might pay off a moderate outstanding mortgage on the family home. It would leave little or nothing to help maintain the family's standard of living. And it would leave little or nothing to meet the cost of college education for any children and to contribute to taking the edge off poverty which would come from exclusive dependence on Social Security checks to

Life Insurance and Personal Income
Per Family in United States

Year	Life Insurance Coverage Per Family	Personal Income Per Family (After Taxes)
1930	$ 2,800	$ 1,900
1935	2,400	1,400
1940	2,700	1,700
1945	3,200	3,200
1950	4,600	4,000
1955	6,900	5,100
1960	10,200	6,100
1961	10,800	6,200
1962	11,400	6,500
1963	12,200	6,700
1964	13,200	7,300
1965	14,600	7,700
1966	15,800	8,200
1967	17,100	8,600
1968	18,300	9,100
1969	19,400	9,500
1970	20,700	10,100
1971	21,700	10,700
1972	22,900	11,300
1973	24,400	12,400
1974	26,500	13,100
1975	28,100	14,100

Sources: *Spectator Year Book*, Institute of Life Insurance,
U.S. Department of Commerce

sustain a widow in her old age. This hardly suggests that the head of an "average" American household can afford the luxury of diverting money from insurance on his life to insurance on the lives of his wife and children.

We might even conclude that the plight of many bereaved American families has been made worse by the extent to which money had been diverted from badly needed insurance against the death of a breadwinner to a savings-insurance fund for children who had a lifetime ahead of them in which to provide for their needs.

This raises the question of how much insurance should be carried by the head of a household, and how does he or she go about determining the amount.

Estimating family needs

We started out with the understanding that the major purpose of life insurance is to insure dependents against economic losses resulting from the death of a breadwinner. The losses might be calculated in terms of the money the head of a family would have earned through his work and investments had he continued living to normal retirement age, say sixty-five. These earnings presumably would have met the costs of maintaining the family's standard of living, helping children through college, and of providing for old age.

It would be difficult to put a dollar figure on the earnings lost as a result of death. It is far more practical and important to estimate the amount of money which the surviving members of the family will need and which no longer can come from earnings of the head of the family. That is the amount which insurance, together with other sources of income, might be expected to provide.

We might first undertake to determine the amount needed to maintain the family until the children are grown, to contribute to their higher education, and to provide for the widow's old age. The figure, of course, will depend on the ages of the surviving dependents, on the number of children, and on the standard of living the family expects to maintain.

Once this figure is secured, we might then estimate how it is to be met. An important contribution can be expected from Social Security. Discounting this amount and any earnings which the widow can rely upon should she undertake employment, the balance represents the amount of money which must be produced by the estate, consisting of insurance benefits and capital in the form of securities, savings, property, and any other interests. Once the value of the capital is estimated, the balance required by the estate can then be calculated as the amount to be covered by insurance.

Three different stages

Let us begin, then, to estimate the needs of a family following the death of the breadwinner. You can establish your own figures while following our hypothetical case of a husband and wife, both age thirty-five, who sat down with pencil and paper to determine the amount she would need for herself and their two children, ten and seven years of age, should he die that year.

They first calculated the monthly income she would need for the first eleven years until the younger child reached age eighteen, and decided it would be about $960 (roughly half the husband's gross income). During this period they estimated that she would receive $625 monthly in Social Security benefits for a widow with two dependent children. That would leave $335 a month for this first stage of eleven years to be covered by the estate.

The second stage covered the period of fourteen years from the time the widow was forty-six until she reached sixty. During this period she would receive no Social Security benefits since she was considered no longer to have dependent children and she had not yet become eligible for a Social Security retirement pension. They estimated that the widow, providing only for herself, could manage with $600 monthly. This amount, over the fourteen-year period of the second stage, would have to be covered entirely by the estate.

The third stage would cover the rest of the widow's life from age sixty, when she would begin to receive monthly Social Security checks of $266. They estimated that she would continue to need about $600 monthly. Deducting the amount received from Social Security, the monthly balance of $334 for the rest of her life would have to be covered by the estate.

The total outlay, excluding income from Social Security,

would be $44,220 in the first stage; $100,800 in the second stage; and, assuming the widow lived until she reached eighty, $80,160 in the third stage. These three figures give us a grand total of $225,180.

However, the estate actually would not have to provide that much money for these living expenses. The total outlay would be made over a period of forty-five years, not all at once, and during that extended period, a large part of the capital of the estate, invested in an annuity and at 5 percent interest, could earn enough so that only $90,624 would be required to meet the living expenses of widow and children.

The summary Table A shows for each of the three periods the monthly amounts required by the widow, provided by Social Security, and allocated by the estate to make up the difference.

Using the tables

We include two tables in this chapter which will help you estimate the amount needed to meet the living costs for a family which has lost its breadwinner. Table I was used by our hypothetical couple to calculate the amount of capital they needed to provide an income of $335 a month for the widow for life. Table II shows the amount of capital, deposited in a savings account paying 5 percent interest annually, required to provide an additional sum of $265 a month for the fourteen years of stage 2.

The reason you need two different tables to solve this problem is the following:

During stage 2, the living costs for the widow were calculated for a definite period of time—fourteen years when the widow, now without dependent children, would lose Social Security benefits and would have to meet the total cost of her expenses from her own resources until Social Security benefits were resumed at age sixty. Table II can be used for estimating the amount of capital required for fixed periods of time.

A different calculation and a different type of table are required to calculate the amount needed to provide an income for an indefinite period. If husband and wife wanted to assume that the widow would live to age eighty, as we did

Table I

Capital You Need to Provide Life Annuity

| AGE OF BENEFICIARY | | Amount Needed to Provide Annuity |
Male	Female*	Per Unit of $10 a Month for Life
25	30	$2,199
30	35	2,152
35	40	2,080
40	45	1,987
45	50	1,894
50	55	1,748
55	60	1,602
60	65	1,425
65	70	1,266
70	75	1,082

*Women's five-year age difference is due to their longer expectation
of life as compared with men.

earlier, they could have estimated an income of $80,160 in the
third stage and they could have used Table II to determine the
amount of capital required to provide that amount. But they
preferred an income for an indefinite period after age sixty.
This calls for a lifetime annuity, which can be issued only by
an insurance company since it involves a sharing of costs and
risks among persons of a given age group, based on the mortality table indicating the average number of years of life
left to each of them. Table I enables us to estimate the amount
of capital required at a given age to provide a lifetime annuity of a given amount of money.

Table B sets down the amount of capital required for each
of the three different periods of living costs to be covered for
our widow with two children. If you have both Tables A and
B at hand, you may more easily follow our explanation of how
we arrived at each figure and then at the total of $90,624
required to meet the total costs involved. Once you see how

Table II

Capital You Need to Provide Income
For Fixed Period

For each unit of $10 of monthly income for the number of years indicated below, you will need the following amounts of money earning 5 percent annual interest, compounded quarterly.

Years	Amount Needed
1	$ 117
2	228
3	334
4	434
5	530
6	621
7	708
8	791
9	869
10	944
11	1,015
12	1,082
13	1,147
14	1,208
15	1,266
16	1,322
17	1,374
18	1,425
19	1,472
20	1,518
21	1,561
22	1,602
23	1,641
24	1,679
25	1,714
26	1,748
27	1,780
28	1,811
29	1,840
30	1,867

the principle operates, you will easily be able to apply it to your own personal case, or those of friends and relatives.

First cover longest period

We begin by establishing first the amount of money needed for the longest period of time and then adding the amount required for the shorter period.

Since the widow requires about $335 a month for the greater part of her life, she could be given an annuity, starting at age thirty-five, to which could be added the additional amount of $265 during stage 2. Table I, our annuity table, enables us to determine how much capital is required to provide a woman, at age thirty-five, with a lifetime monthly income of $335. The cost for each unit of $10 a month is $2,152. Since we need $335 a month, we require 33.5 units. Multiplied by $2,152, we get a total of $72,092 as the amount of capital required for the first step in our calculation.

Beginning at age forty-six, she will need a monthly increment of $265 for fourteen years to raise to $600 the monthly amount required during the period there will be no Social Security income. Turning to Table II, we find that, for a period of fourteen years, $1,208 is the amount needed to provide a monthly unit income of $10. To provide $265 monthly, we need 26.5 times $1,208, or a total of $32,012. Since $32,012 is not required until eleven years after her husband's death, $18,532.39, deposited at 5 percent interest compounded quarterly, would produce the amount needed.

Adding together the two amounts of capital required, we reach the total capital requirement of $90,624 shown in Table B. This amount of capital will take care of the largest and most important area of expenditure—namely, the day-to-day cost of living which a widow must be able to meet for herself and children. Unfortunately, there are additional sums to be taken into account, as shown in the summary, Table C.

Allocating other funds

Our hypothetical couple, representing a well-educated segment of our middle class, will want to provide a fund for the higher education of their two children. They decide to allocate $8,000 to each child, bearing in mind that each will be eligible

Table A

Lifetime Living Expenses for Widow, 35, With Two Children, 10 and 7

Period	Monthly Income Required	Monthly Social Security (Estimated)	Monthly Amount To Be Provided By Estate
I. 11 years, until younger child reaches 18; widow reaches 46	$960	$625	$335
II. 14 years, widow, between ages of 46 and 60 no longer receives Social Security benefits	$600	none	$600
III. Rest of widow's life from age 60, without dependent children	$600	$266	$334

Table B

Capital Needed for Living Expenses For Widow With Two Children

Period	Monthly Income	Capital Required
I. Lifetime	$335	$72,092
II. 14 years (widow 46 to 60)	$265	$18,532
Total capital required		$90,624

Table C

Estate Budget
For Widow and Two Children

	Capital Required	
I. Living expenses, widow and children	$ 90,624	
II. College fund for two children	16,000	
III. Liquidation of mortgage	15,000	
IV. Emergency fund	5,000	
Total capital needs	$126,624	$126,624
Assets available		20,000
Amount to be covered by insurance		$106,624

for continued Social Security support while going to college between the ages of eighteen and twenty-two, even though their mother will cease to receive her benefit when the younger child reaches eighteen.

To relieve the family of the burden of continuing to service the mortgage on their house, they list $15,000 as the amount required to liquidate the outstanding obligation to the bank.

Finally, they enter a sum of $5,000 as the amount which should be available for readjustment, following the death of the husband, and other emergencies.

The total of these requirements comes to the grand sum of $126,624. The couple estimates that they can count on $20,000 of assets, representing savings, stocks, and group life insurance maintained by his company. This leaves a balance of $106,624 to be covered by life insurance.

The important question now relates to the best and least expensive way of financing this amount of insurance. This is the subject of our next chapter.

Before closing this one, however, it might be worthwhile to summarize the steps we have taken in order to establish the amount of insurance required for the hypothetical case we have used as a guide for our readers. We might also add a few lines about Social Security in view of the important contribution its benefits can make toward a widow with dependent children.

Summarizing the steps

To determine the amount of insurance required to protect a family against the economic loss resulting from the death of a breadwinner, we take the following steps:

1. Establish the monthly income required by a widow with children for a reasonable standard of living.

2. Deduct amounts receivable from Social Security and private pension funds to determine the monthly deficit to be filled by the estate.

3. Estimate the amount of capital required to produce the income expected from the estate.

4. Total the principal amounts of capital required to achieve major objectives, including those needed to produce income for living expenses of widow and children, to liquidate the mortgage on the house, to establish a college fund for children, and to provide an emergency fund.

5. Deduct the total of various assets, including the value of savings, securities, property (other than the house), business interests, and company group life insurance.

6. The balance represents the amount to be covered by insurance. If this figure is greater than the amount of insurance you are carrying at present, the difference indicates the amount of additional insurance required to cover the expenditure envisaged. If the figure is smaller, you may be carrying too much insurance for the future income required.

In view of constantly changing circumstances, it is advisable periodically to review the current and future needs of a family to determine whether more or less insurance protection is required. As families increase in size, so does the need for greater protection. As children reach their majority, the need for protection—and insurance—may decrease.

The benefits of Social Security

The public generally associates Social Security with retirement benefits beginning at the age of sixty-two or sixty-five.

It appears to have lost sight of the fact that one of the program's most important functions—and one of its major expenditures—relates to support of widowed mothers with dependent children. Assuming her husband had been properly covered by Social Security, a widow, regardless of age, and her dependent children are entitled to so-called survivors' benefits. These benefits could total as much as $180,000. By referring to Table I, you can estimate the great amount of capital required to produce such an amount of money over any given period of time.

Most employed and self-employed persons are covered by Social Security. Employees of the federal government are covered by separate programs outside the scope of the Social Security system. In both cases, employees and their employers contribute to the programs. In the case of Social Security, an employee's annual earnings up to $15,300 are subject to a 5.85 percent tax. The amount is deducted from paychecks and is matched by equal contributions from employers. Participation in the program is compulsory, and an employee cannot legally escape paying what is widely regarded as an additional tax on his income—that is, additional to the federal income tax which also is deducted before the employee sees his paycheck.

Social Security can be regarded as a combination of life insurance, providing payments to widows and children, disability insurance, and a retirement program. There are differences of opinion as to whether benefits from the government program are better than or inferior to those which could be secured from private companies for each dollar paid by employee and employer. The amount deducted from an employee's salary can be considered to be similar to a premium payment for insurance. Those earning at least $15,300 annually are now paying $895.05 annually to Social Security. With the equal sum paid by the employer, the annual "premium" being paid into the account of each employee comes to $1,790.10. This is many times more than what the "average" American is paying for insurance with private companies and has become the major insurance investment as well as the major source of insurance protection of most Americans.

Eligibility rules

There are several rules that govern the period you must work in a covered occupation before your family becomes eligible for benefits. As a general rule, if you have worked in an occupation covered by Social Security over a year and a half, your family will be eligible for survivors' benefits. As the law puts it, you will be "currently insured" if you have at least six quarters of coverage in the thirteen-quarter period ending with the quarter in which you die. A quarter of coverage is defined as a calendar quarter in which an individual is paid $50 or more in wages in covered employment or is credited with at least $400 of self-employment income (which counts for four quarters).

The surviving widow of an eligible worker will receive monthly benefits under the Social Security Act if she has one or more children under the age of eighteen or a disabled child of any age. Benefits will also be paid to the children until they reach age eighteen, or to age twenty-two if they are in full-time attendance at an accredited school or college. When a child reaches eighteen, or twenty-two if at school, his benefits cease. The widow's Social Security support terminates when she no longer has a child under the age of eighteen. It is resumed, as a retirement benefit, when she reaches age sixty. It is important to note that a widow's benefit terminates when her youngest child reaches the age of eighteen, even though the child may continue to receive his benefit until he is twenty-two by virtue of being a full-time student.

The size of the monthly income that will be paid to the widow and dependent children of a covered worker will depend on the average earnings of the worker during his covered lifetime, as well as the length of time for which deductions were made from his wages towards his Social Security account. The table on page 45 gives the monthly benefits payable to a widow with two children below the age of eighteen when her husband dies in 1976. The amount of the benefit varies with the age of the husband at the time of his death. The table cites benefits at several ages, all based on the assumption that the husband, throughout his working years, was earning at least the maximum on which Social

Social Security Benefits
For Widow and Children
(Effective June, 1976)

Age of Worker At Time of His Death in 1976	Maximum Monthly Income Payable to Widow With Two Children Under Age 18
47-61	$680.40
44	708.80
39	767.40
34	831.70
29 or under	959.40

Maximum Income Taxable for Social Security

Years	Maximum Income Levels
1951 through 1954	$ 3,600
1955 through 1958	4,200
1959 through 1965	4,800
1966 and 1967	6,600
1968 through 1971	7,800
1972	9,000
1973	10,800
1974	13,200
1975	14,100
1976	15,300

Maximum Social Security Benefits for Widow
(Effective June, 1976)

Age of Worker at Time of His Death	Monthly Benefit to Widow Commencing at Age 60	Age 65
47-61	$271.60	$379.80
44	288.30	403.10
39	313.60	438.60
34	339.80	475.20
29 or under	392.00	548.20

Security taxes were paid and benefits computed. (The table at the bottom of page 45 sets forth these amounts.)

Widow's wages affect benefits

It is also important to note that the benefits payable to a widow will be reduced if she earns more than $2,760 in a year. Her benefit (but *not* the benefits of the surviving children) will usually be reduced by $1 for each $2 she earns in excess of $2,760 during a year. However, no matter how much she earns in a year, she can get her full benefit for any month in which she does not earn more than $230. These rules apply to widows under the age of seventy-two. The payments to the dependent children will *not* be affected by the fact that their mother's earnings in any year made her ineligible to receive her full benefits.

No payments are made to a widow without dependent children before she reaches age sixty unless she is disabled, in which case she is entitled to a reduced benefit any time between ages fifty and sixty. If she waits until she is sixty-five, she will receive her full benefits.

Retirement benefits are available to the widow of a covered worker when she reaches age sixty, whether or not she previously had received survivors' benefits when her children were below eighteen. As in the case of a widow with children under eighteen in her care, the widow's benefit when she reaches age sixty depends on the earnings of her husband and the number of years during which deductions were made towards Social Security.

Again assuming that up to the time of his death the worker was earning the maximums on which benefits were computed over the past twenty-six years (see the table on page 45) and that he died in 1976, the table on page 46 lists a widow's benefits beginning at age sixty and, alternatively, at age sixty-five.

In this instance, too, her benefits will be reduced $1 for each $2 she earns in a year above the $2,760 figure. After age seventy-two, there is no further restriction on the amount she may earn from employment. Such deductions, which do not apply to income from savings and investments, have created bitter resentment on the part of those who feel they are being penalized for trying to lift themselves above a Social Security subsistence level by working for additional income.

For further details about Social Security benefits, you might consult a concise and easy-to-understand booklet, available free of charge from the United States Department of Health, Education, and Welfare, Social Security Administration, Washington, D.C. 20025. Any questions as to your eligibility for benefits and the size of these benefits may also be discussed in person at any field office of the Social Security Administration. If you cannot locate in the telephone book the address of the office nearest your home, your local post office will direct you to it.

3

More Coverage for Less Money

A rich man may be able to provide for his dependents without insurance. The wealth he commands, assuming it is relatively secure and liquid, could serve as his insurance.

The man of moderate or modest means, precisely because he does not command much wealth, hardly has any choice but to depend on insurance to protect his family against an untimely loss of his earnings. Since his funds are limited and his liabilities may be great, he might be expected to seek the maximum amount of coverage for the least amount of money. Yet, as often as not, such is not the case. The reason is that many are confused by the multiplicity of policies on the market and an inability to choose between them on the basis of price and quality.

One of the major reasons for the confusion, as indicated earlier, is due to the fact that there are two strikingly different classes and philosophies of insurance—term and cash value. It is not easy to compare the costs of these two types of policies because, year after year, the cost relationship between the two keeps changing. As the savings element in the cash-value policy multiplies with time, it appears to gain an advantage over the term policy.

Mutual and stock companies

Confusion is compounded by the fact that policies are offered by two different kinds of companies operating under different principles. Stock companies, which operate to produce a profit for their stockholders, mostly offer policies at a fixed cost. Mutual companies, which technically belong to the holders of their policies, offer participation in their profits.

The mutual company issues an annual "dividend" which can be deducted from the annual premium; the stock company issues no dividend. Thus the cost of "participating policies" (or "par" policies) issued by "participating companies" cannot be established and compared with those of "nonparticipating" (or "nonpar") policies issued by stock companies until after the dividend, if any, is determined and declared. However, estimates of dividends are made on the basis of amounts issued by mutual companies over a period of years, and these figures, "not guaranteed," are cited for the benefit of the insurance buyer when cost comparisons between par and nonpar policies are to be made.

The annual premium of a participating policy often is higher than that of a nonparticipating policy, but after the dividend is declared and deducted, the cost may—or may not—be less. This requires the insurance buyer to make a close comparison between par and nonpar policies as well as between cash-value and term policies.

In order to draw a comparison with the cost of a term policy which carries no cash values, we must also establish the "net cost" of the cash-value policy. In the case of the participating policies, this is achieved by deducting dividends and cash values from premium payments over a period of years and then striking an average figure. In the case of nonparticipating policies, a similar average is drawn after deducting the cash values. Term is the simplest to calculate, an average being made of the premium costs over a period of years for a comparable amount of insurance coverage.

The illustrative examples and tables included in this chapter are intended to assist the reader in making his own evaluations as between the different kinds of policies on the basis of figures which insurance salesmen can be called upon to deliver. Premium prices for one-year and five-year term insurance and ordinary (permanent, whole-life) cash-value insurance, published in the appendix, may also prove useful as a guide to what are considered to be among the highest and the lowest prices for these different policies.

The chances are that a comparison of premium prices for specific companies would be outdated by the time it was printed. For current prevailing rates, the reader should call upon his insurance agent or the companies in which he is interested. These rates might then be checked against the high-low limits listed in the appendix.

It is important to note that policies cannot be selected on the basis of cost alone. Some contain special features, such as a waiver of premiums in case of disability, whereas others do not. Whether you are considering lower- or higher-cost policies, it is advisable to take into account the qualitative provisions of the contract.

In the various examples which follow we have used relatively modest amounts of insurance—between $10,000 and $50,000. These can be used as a guide to the costs of greater amounts which may be of interest to the reader. However, it should be noted that higher amounts of insurance are often available at "discount rates," and this aspect, too, should be taken into account when dealing with insurance agents and companies.

Term insurance costs less

The tables, figures, and examples indicate that a given amount of insurance coverage is provided at a lower cost by term insurance than by cash-value insurance, particularly in earlier years. Put another way, a man in his thirties can buy at least three times more protection by selecting term rather than cash-value insurance.

In the preceding chapter, our hypothetical couple calculated that they would need $106,624 of insurance to build up an estate which would support a widow for the rest of her life, enable her to maintain their two children until they reached college age, contribute to their higher education, and meet emergencies. That amount at first seemed forbidding.

Examining his budget, the man found that he could allocate only $330 to life insurance each year. If he were to buy nonpar ordinary life, at the relatively low rate of about $17 per thousand dollars of insurance, he would secure roughly $20,000 worth of coverage.

On the other hand, were he to choose nonpar five-year renewable and convertible term, available at a low-level rate of about $3.09 per thousand dollars, he could secure nearly $107,000 of insurance—the amount he needs for the adequate protection of his family.

The choice was between inadequate coverage, with promise of increasing cash values should he live long enough, and adequate coverage without such promise.

If the couple could afford to carry the coverage they needed on a cash-value basis, they would not have had a problem. They might have had the best of both worlds—protection and savings of cash values within an ordinary, whole-life policy.

However, even in this case, they might have hesitated before committing all their money to cash-value. Had the larger amount of money been available, they might have followed the principle which has become known as "buy term and bank the difference." This means that, at a fraction of the cost of cash-value insurance, they might have bought term to give them the coverage they needed and invested the difference (between the cost of term and cash value) in a savings account at 5 percent compound interest or better. The tables show that such a principle promises a better form of savings than does that of a cash-value policy.

The paramount problem in this case, however, was adequate insurance coverage rather than long-term savings, and the only way this couple could solve it was to buy term insurance. As time went on and the need for insurance coverage became less acute, the couple would be able to trim back the amount of term they would need, and they could either invest the difference in a savings account, in securities which might offer an even greater return, or in a moderate amount of cash-value insurance which would provide coverage beyond age sixty, when the cost of term insurance becomes prohibitive.

The conclusion which might be drawn from the example of our hypothetical couple is that term insurance offers greater coverage than cash-value insurance for young families which need the greatest possible amount of coverage at the lowest cost. While the cost of term appears to increase more rapidly than that of ordinary insurance in older years, the need for coverage may also have decreased with the passage of time so that the burden of carrying a smaller amount of term need not be much greater than it was before.

In short, the decision seems to hinge on whether the head of a family, taking into account the amount of coverage required to protect his family, can afford the risk of cutting back on insurance so as to increase his savings program, or whether the highly desirable goal of increased savings should be sacrificed to the necessity of adequate coverage against the uncertainties of each successive day.

That savings should be handled as separate and distinct from insurance protection was advocated as far back as ninety years ago by the then insurance commissioner of Massachusetts, John K. Tarbox. In his official report in 1884, he said: "A provident person will do wiser to buy his insurance of an insurance company and make his deposits, if he wishes to make investments of that character, with some regular savings institutions whose sole business is the administration of trust funds. To unite more than need be for the assurance of its contracts the proper business of an insurance company with the function of a savings bank makes a combination that is both incongruous and unwise."

Accumulating savings in policy

Many policyholders insist that the only savings they ever accumulate is in their life insurance policies. "When it comes to putting money in the bank," the argument goes,

"I always find something better to do with it. But when I've got to get up my life insurance premium, I always manage somehow, if I have to beg, borrow, or steal."

Proponents of life insurance as a form of compulsory savings point to statistics showing that large groups of wage earners have no sizable savings outside of the reserves in their life insurance policies. The inference is that if they had no life insurance, or if they had purchased low-cost term insurance which develops no cash values, they would not have even the little financial security afforded by the cash or loan values of their insurance policies.

It is true that those who cannot save money will not be able to use term insurance to their best advantage. However, advocates of term insurance do not believe that every person who manages with some effort to meet his annual premiums for high-cost insurance would necessarily spend any difference he might save under low-cost plans. It is possible that some persons spending, say, $284 for $10,000 of life insurance (twenty-payment life at age thirty-five) are not saving money precisely because of the size of the outlay for their insurance. If they had purchased this same amount of insurance on the term plan for a fraction of the cost, the money they saved might have found its way into some form of thrift. Another form of "compulsory" savings, of course, would be regular payroll deductions which are deposited to a savings or bond-purchasing account.

The discipline of the life insurance premium notice is sometimes said to be most effective for persons in the lower income group. However, in this group particularly, the amount of life insurance is severely limited by the cost of the premium.

For these persons to buy insurance at more than the lowest possible rate has the effect of reducing the already limited provisions they can afford, often with tragic consequences. Also, it is this income group, more than any other, which is most threatened by loss due to early withdrawal from high-premium insurance.

Danger of policy termination

Whatever your income bracket, the danger of early termi-

nation of insurance is quite real. Statistics on termination
of policies—on the small percentage of policies that are
paid as death claims or carried to maturity—can be interpreted at great length. But you can get some idea of the
odds against your holding a policy over long periods of time
from the figures on lapsed life insurance.

The most widely used published figures on terminations
are those developed by the late actuary M. Albert Linton.
Three sets of basic lapse statistics are given: Linton A.
(lowest lapses); Linton B (medium range); and Linton C
(highest). According to the medium-range figures (Linton
B), 20 percent of all newly purchased life insurance policies
are discontinued in their first year. An additional 12 percent
do not continue beyond their second year; 10 percent terminate in the third year; and 8.8 percent and 8 percent in
their fourth and fifth years, respectively. The Linton A table
presents a brighter picture but even under this set of statistics, only 75.1 percent of all policies are paid for five full years.

"Life insurance account"

The forced-savings value of permanent insurance should be
weighed against the advantages of low-cost term insurance. If
you find yourself dependent on the thrift discipline of the
high-premium policy, you might consider a special account
in a savings institution which you earmark as your "life
insurance account." While carrying only low-cost term insurance, you could make regular deposits into this fund
large enough to pay for high-premium insurance. You could
deduct the premiums for your insurance from this account,
leaving the balance to accumulate at interest.

Thus, if you find that you need $20,000 of life insurance
to cover your needs, you will be able to choose from a variety of plans ranging in cost at age thirty-five from $61.80
annually for five-year renewable term to $340.80 annually
for a whole-life policy. If your first step is to take care of
your life insurance needs at the lowest possible cost, you
would buy $20,000 of renewable term insurance for about
$61.80 a year for the first five years. At the same time, you
would take stock of your finances and conclude that you can
"spend" about $750 a year on life insurance and savings.

You could then put the $750 into a savings fund each year and use this fund to pay life insurance premiums. You could even have your bank issue a check to the order of the life insurance company when the premium falls due on your policy. In this way, you would learn to think of the annual deposit of $750 as a regular "obligation." You would be saving regularly at the same time as you provide for your life insurance needs on a low-cost, flexible basis.

A plan of separate savings and insurance covered by one payment is available to residents of Massachusetts, New York, and Connecticut, and to persons who are employed in those states. Life insurance is sold in the three states at attractive rates directly to the insured at mutual savings banks, but in Connecticut there is a $5,000 maximum on the amount of ordinary insurance that can be purchased. A qualified person may open a regular savings account in one of these banks and authorize deduction of premiums on insurance purchased in the bank's life insurance department. In this way, it is possible to carry low-cost term insurance and create a growing cash fund outside of a policy—both with one regular deposit.

Some of these banks advertise a life-savings plan, or packaged savings, or some similarly titled combination of insurance and a savings account for a set weekly or monthly deposit.

In these three states, the procedure for building a life insurance estate and a separate savings fund is quite simple to the extent at least that banks are authorized to sell life insurance.

A program of separate savings and life insurance could make it possible for you to accomplish the following objectives:

1. Capitalize your future earnings at the lowest possible cost. In this way, you could attain or at least approximate the full life insurance estate you require.

2. Avoid the severe losses which attend early termination of level-premium policies, when you find it necessary to discontinue a policy in its early years.

3. Preserve the flexibility of your life insurance program, which can be decreased without loss as your needs change.

4. Avoid burdensome premium loads which threaten your entire insurance estate with breakdown.

A method of saving

Even if you require no life insurance to safeguard dependents, an insurance salesman may urge you to use the policy as a method of regular savings. He will demonstrate that your money will be invested with virtually no risk and, at the end of a given period of years, you will receive a fruitful "yield" on your premiums. For such purposes, either whole life or some form of endowment policy may be offered, the latter accumulating the larger cash fund per dollar deposited. When you total the amount of premiums you agree to pay in a given period, you find that your policy guarantees the return of a sum of money which is larger than the "cost" of the insurance, at least at the younger ages. This is referred to as "return over cost," and provides inducement for considering the endowment policy an adequate means of regular accumulation of savings.

To see how effectively an insurance policy can provide a method of regular savings, we need only compare the performance of a policy of the kind recommended for this purpose with that of a straight savings or investment plan. Endowment policies can be bought for various periods but the usual type is the twenty-year endowment, which is the one used in our comparison, issued by a leading insurance company.

Under this type of policy, if the insured person dies before the twentieth year, his beneficiary is paid the full insurance. If the insured person is alive at the end of the twentieth year, then he collects the full amount of the insurance.

Against the accumulation in the twenty-year endowment policy, we shall compare deposits of equal sums in a regular savings account earning 5 percent interest. The type of accumulation we are considering—regular deposits over a long period of years—can be expected to secure earnings of 5 percent without speculative risks. United States Savings Bonds, Series E, will do even better, providing a yield of approximately 6 percent when held for five years.

Savings methods compared

In the table on page 58 we compare a $10,000 twenty-year endowment policy issued at age twenty-five with savings accumulating at 5 percent. In this savings fund we deposit the same amount as we would pay for the annual premium to the insurance company—namely, $440. The second column of figures shows the amount of cash available to you in your policy at the end of each year. The third column shows the funds accumulated by depositing equal sums each year in a savings account yielding 5 percent interest. All figures are shown to the nearest dollar.

As you can see, even at the end of twenty years, the endowment policy "yields" $5,276 less than straight savings earning 5 percent.

It should be pointed out that there are several variables, and changes in these factors would affect the results. Thus, the cash values during the policy term would differ slightly in other companies; "participating" policies (those of mutual companies and of stock companies which issue participating insurance) would show up differently from the "nonparticipating" contract used in our example (that of a nonmutual—or stock company—which issues no dividends) ; and a different age at issue than age twenty-five or a policy of a different amount than $10,000 would affect the figures. But none of these could cancel the very substantial advantage accruing to the straight savings account.

Of more substance in its effect on our figures is the difference in the tax treatment of these two types of accumulation. Life insurance cash values enjoy a considerable advantage in that they are not subject to income tax except in those cases where they exceed the sum of the premiums paid for the policy, and then only when the policy is cashed in. The individual accumulating his money in a savings bank would be liable for income taxes on all the interest his money earned. The table on page 59 reflects the tax effect on the two programs.

The superiority of the straight savings plan is reduced, as might be expected, when income taxes are taken into account, but the savings plan is still $5,058 ahead.

While both tables compare the cash values in an endowment

How Cash Values in Endowment Policy With $440 Annual Premium Compare With Annual Savings Deposits of $440 *Before* Taxes

End of Year	Cash Values In Policy	In Savings Deposits at 5% Interest Compounded Annually
1	$ 100	$ 462
2	490	947
3	890	1,456
4	1,300	1,991
5	1,730	2,553
6	2,170	3,142
7	2,620	3,762
8	3,090	4,412
9	3,570	5,094
10	4,070	5,811
11	4,580	6,564
12	5,110	7,354
13	5,660	8,183
14	6,220	9,055
15	6,800	9,969
16	7,400	10,930
17	8,020	11,938
18	8,660	12,997
19	9,320	14,109
20	10,000	15,276

Note: Nonparticipating policy for male age 25.

How Cash Values in Endowment Policy With $440 Annual Premium Compare With Annual Savings Deposits of $440 *After* Taxes

End of Year	Cash Values In Policy	In Savings Deposits at 5% Interest Compounded Annually
1	$ 100	$ 455
2	490	934
3	890	1,436
4	1,300	1,963
5	1,730	2,516
6	2,170	3,098
7	2,620	3,708
8	3,090	4,349
9	3,570	5,021
10	4,070	5,728
15	6,800	9,827
20	10,000	15,058

Note: Nonparticipating policy for male age 25 in 30 percent income tax bracket.

policy with annual savings deposits of an amount equal to the
annual policy premium, they do not take into account the fact
that the $440 annual premium covers life insurance protec-
tion as well as savings. Making allowances for the life insurance coverage in the endowment policy, the bank savings
would still come out ahead of cash values in the insurance policy except possibly for persons in higher income tax brackets.

Early withdrawal loss

To look at the differences between the two plans only at
the end of the twentieth year is to leave out of consideration
the much greater differences at any point during the twenty-
year period. If you should be forced to withdraw from the
endowment policy before the end of twenty years, the loss
involved when compared to the straight 5 percent savings
investment is much more marked. A glance at the table on
page 58 will show how severe is the difference in any
earlier year. Early withdrawal from the insurance plan is
thus seen to be subject to "penalty," in comparison with the
savings plan, where your full deposits plus interest are available at any time. This factor is of the utmost importance in
appraising any life insurance contract undertaken solely as
a means of saving, where no actual life insurance protection is indicated.

Elaborate statistics have been compiled to show how small
is the percentage of policies that are carried to maturity,
and hotly contested interpretations are put on these figures.
Whatever the arguments, there is a very real possibility that
a policyholder may be compelled or may want to discontinue
a policy before the end of twenty years. It is important,
therefore, not only to compare the sums accumulated after
long periods of time but also to remember that early withdrawal from any life insurance plan undertaken solely as a
method of saving is commonly attended by losses.

Some argue that term insurance, though lowest in premium, is actually the most expensive of all plans when you
figure "how much you get back." This analysis arrives at
the "net cost" of a whole-life policy by totaling all the premiums you pay over a long period of time, usually twenty
years, and deducting from this outlay all the dividends that

"Net" Costs of Whole-Life vs. Term

The table shows the advantage of a whole-life policy over term insurance if the buyer of term does not invest his savings differential. Investing the differential could have the effect of giving the term-insurance buyer a lower cost over the 20-year period than that of the buyer of whole life. The whole-life insurance in the example is a $10,000 nonparticipating policy for a man age 35. For purpose of simplification, interest on savings in the cash-value policy is not taken into account.

	Whole Life	5-Year Term
	Annual Premium $191.10 payable for 20 years	Annual Premium $65.40 payable for first 5 years
		$81.10 payable for second 5 years
		$105.80 payable for third 5 years
		$149.00 payable for last 5 years
Total premiums paid	$3,822.00	$2,006.50
Less cash surrender value	3,420.00	none
Total cost for 20 years	$ 402.00	$2,006.50
Annual cost	20.10	100.32
Annual cost per $1,000	2.01	10.03

you may expect to receive during that time from a mutual life insurance company. The difference represents the money that you "paid out" for the policy. Since you can surrender your policy and receive a cash sum, the cash surrender value is then deducted from the total payments you made. The difference between the outgoing and incoming money is called the "net cost" of the policy to you.

This net cost is used to make comparisons between different policies of the same company as well as those of competing companies. On the basis of the comparative net costs of the two policies in the table on page 61, the term policy appears to be the most expensive, five times as high in this instance.

All these savings are predicated upon your living to the end of twenty years. If death intervenes before the end of the twentieth year, which is the time the lower net-cost economies are secured, the whole-life policy would cost much more than the term insurance. Thus, if death occurs during the first year, the whole-life policy will have called for premiums about three times as high as the term policy— $191.10 as opposed to $65.40.

Two policies compared

However, let us assume that you will survive the next twenty years, and let us compare the two policies to ascertain the real differences in cost. The whole-life and the five-year renewable term policies to be compared in this analysis are both nonpar policies issued by the same company. While the figures would differ somewhat for similar policies of another company, for policies of different amounts, or for those issued at another age, the intrinsic value of the analysis will apply with like validity.

For purposes of the comparison, assume that you and your neighbor are both age thirty-five and require life insurance estates of the same size. You buy $10,000 of whole life for an annual premium of $191.10. Your neighbor buys five-year renewable term for a premium of $65.40—$125.70 less than you are paying. He deposits this difference in a savings account earning 5 percent interest. From the first year, your neighbor can provide an "estate" as large as

Cash in Whole-Life Policy
vs.
Cash in Savings Account

The following table compares cash values in a $10,000 nonparticipating whole-life policy with deposits in a bank at 5 percent compounded interest before taxes, which are made with savings derived from buying $10,000 of 5-year nonparticipating term insurance instead of whole-life and decreasing it as the savings fund grows so that the total of decreasing term and increasing savings always is $10,000. Both insured persons begin at age 35.

End of Year	In $10,000 Whole-Life Policy	In Savings Fund While Carrying Term Insurance
1	none	$ 133
2	none	272
3	$ 160	420
5	480	740
10	1,370	1,633
15	2,350	2,703
20	3,420	4,027

Note: All figures to nearest dollar.

yours, with only $9,874 of insurance. For in the event of his death, his beneficiary would receive $9,874 from his insurance policy and the savings deposit of $125.70—a total of $9,999.70.

The following year, your premium under your whole-life policy remains the same, while your neighbor's outside savings fund has grown because of the 5 percent interest being credited to it. The amount of insurance he now requires to achieve an estate of $10,000 will be less than it was the previous year, and will cost him only $64.53. Again, as in the first year, this premium is smaller than your $191.10

and your neighbor deposits the difference in premiums in his savings fund. His combined estate is still exactly as large as yours—$10,000. Each year, your neighbor continues this process of decreasing the amount of insurance he carries to keep pace with the growth of his savings. All through this period, you maintain your $10,000 whole-life policy. At all times, your outlay for insurance is exactly the same as your neighbor's, and the estates you have each set up are identical.

At the end of twenty years, you can surrender your whole-life policy and receive the cash value. Your neighbor's term policy has no cash value, but he has accumulated a fund in his savings account. The table on page 63 shows the cash available to you and your neighbor at different intervals during the twenty years.

Your neighbor will have accumulated more money than you at every point, including the end of the twentieth year. Calculated this way, your neighbor's term insurance program is more economical than the one shown under the "net cost" comparison on page 61.

The differences between your available cash and your neighbor's at any point during the twenty-year period might also be considered. If you should be forced to cease making payments on your policy, or should desire to do so for any reason, the differences between your neighbor's funds and yours will be noteworthy, especially in the early years. The table on page 63 shows that for the first two years, you have no cash value at all, while your neighbor has $272 at the end of the second year. At the end of the third year, your neighbor's $420 compares with the $160 in your policy. At the fifth year, his accumulation is $740; yours is $480. Even as late as the tenth year, his $1,633 is over 19 percent better than your $1,370. It is obvious that early withdrawal from the plan involves "penalties" which your neighbor avoids under his term insurance and separate savings plan.

Effect of taxes

The cash-value increments in life insurance policies, being relatively tax free, enjoy a considerable advantage over most other forms of savings or investment. Thus, when you surrender your whole-life policy at the end of twenty years, there would be virtually no income tax to pay. Your neighbor, on the other hand, would have been taxed each year on the interest being credited to his savings account. This favored tax status of cash values in life insurance would affect our comparison to the extent that the interest in your neighbor's savings account is reduced by taxes. The amount of the reduction would depend on his income tax bracket.

It has been estimated that savings of a term policyholder at 3½ percent interest *after* taxes would be greater than the tax-free cash values in an ordinary life policy throughout the period of comparison until after age sixty, when insurance cash values would overtake the savings account. If the term policyholder were able to invest his savings at a net return of 6 percent after taxes, his saving account would remain considerably ahead of the insurance tax values.

Policies evaluated

We might conclude with a brief resume and evaluation of term as compared with cash-value insurance.

The difficulty in making a judgment about life insurance, as pointed out, is due to the large variety of available policies, different kinds of companies offering them (par and nonpar), and considerable confusion over the element of "savings" in ordinary, whole-life, or other cash-value policies.

When life insurance first was developed, it took the form of "pure" insurance, such as fire or any other kind of risk covered by insurance. With the mortality table ceaselessly driving up the cost of coverage year after year, policyholders found it increasingly difficult to meet their premium payments and to retain their coverage. Necessity being the mother of invention, a brilliant idea was born to solve the problem. The idea was to establish "level" premiums by having the policyholder make overpayments in the earlier years of his life so that in the later years he would be able to continue making the same payments and he would be spared the pain of the prohibitively high premiums caused by the inexorable march of mortality. The overpayments of the earlier years, together with the interest they earned, would meet the higher costs of the later years.

Notwithstanding this stroke of genius, insurance salesmen continued to find resistance on the part of potential
buyers who were put off by the idea of paying for a whole-
life policy for their entire lives and never seeing any return
on their money while they lived. Permanent insurance was
then regarded as "death" insurance—payable upon death to
someone else. In an attempt to present permanent insurance
in a more attractive light, salesmen began to develop the
"positive" values of insurance which the policyholder could
enjoy during his lifetime—namely, the cash values. They
observed that these cash values represented a form of savings which the policyholder could always draw upon in an
emergency or keep for his retirement. And they also stressed
the point that these cash values could be used as collateral
for loans. It was this emphasis on the "savings" quality of
cash values that has created the problem of putting the
cash values of permanent insurance into proper perspective.

If these cash values are regarded as an overpayment for
a special fund which makes it possible to maintain level-
premium payments and to avoid painfully high premiums
in later years, then they should not be considered in the
same light as a savings account in a bank. While cash values
may be savings, they are savings for a specific purpose—to
meet the higher premium costs of later years. If these cash
values are drawn upon, then the specific purpose for which
they were created is being defeated. Thus borrowing against
cash values in a life insurance policy is quite different from
withdrawing or borrowing against deposits in a savings
account. The former may damage a long-term financing program for permanent life insurance. The latter may not be
related to life insurance in any way.

That is why some insurance agents strongly urge their
clients not to touch their cash values except in cases of
emergency, and then to replace the borrowed money as soon
as they can.

Finding the best solution
With this better perspective of permanent insurance in
mind, we might then recapitulate the merits of the two different kinds of insurance. Term insurance is particularly

useful in earlier years when the cost is relatively low so that the head of a growing family, with heavy responsibilities, can secure much more coverage than would be available to him if he were to buy higher-cost permanent insurance. As his need for coverage decreases in later life, when the cost of term becomes much more expensive, he may be able to offset these higher costs by reducing the amount of his term insurance.

However, this would not take care of the problem of continued insurance for the later years of his life, or for the whole of his life. As mentioned frequently, the cost of term becomes prohibitive in later years—so much so that there is virtually no demand for term after age sixty-five. Ordinary life, then, becomes the most practical way of securing permanent insurance for the later years of a policyholder's life.

This brings us to the problem of meeting the cost in later years, which is extremely high for ordinary life as well as for term. And the solution to the problem is to secure some ordinary life insurance in earlier years so as to take advantage of the level-premium feature which it offers.

The ideal arrangement, then, appears to be a mixture of both term and permanent insurance—term to take care of the heavy coverage required during the early years of a growing family and permanent insurance to take care of the reduced needs of later years, yet at a premium cost which would not prove too burdensome. The relative amounts as between these two kinds of insurance would depend, of course, on the particular needs and circumstances of the individual.

A third element which might enter into the ideal arrangement would be a separate savings and investment account. The savings account would provide accumulations for longer term investment and would be available to meet emergencies without forcing the policyholder to draw down the cash values of his permanent insurance. Thus, the wise family financial planner is the one who can make the best allocation of funds as between the three elements of the equation—term, ordinary life insurance, and savings.

4

Tips
for Buying
Term

While term insurance holds its attractions, as pointed out in earlier chapters, it also has its limitations. One of the most serious is that, in most cases, it is not renewed beyond age sixty-five, so that those who feel the need of some continued coverage beyond that age must look elsewhere. The answer, of course, is to be found in ordinary, whole-life permanent insurance, and the challenge to the economy-minded insurance buyer is how to secure the best of both worlds—term and whole life. This calls for moving carefully, with both eyes open, so as to avoid pitfalls in the course of combining these two different types of coverage into an overall, economic insurance program.

We might first take up the argument, often advanced by salesmen with a greater interest in signing cash-value contracts, that term is only "temporary" insurance and cannot serve the purpose of "permanent" insurance. The argument that it is "temporary" can be disposed of with recognition of the fact that term insurance, by being renewed periodically, can become "permanent" up to age sixty-five. And if more "permanence" is required after that age, then the term policy might be converted to a whole-life policy, at a considerably higher cost, of course, since whole life, including cash values, must be more expensive than term, which is "pure" insurance without the cash value savings element attached to it.

However, considerable care must be exercised to be sure that term can be continued to age sixty-five and that it can be converted after that to a cash-value type of insurance. Most companies write one or more varieties of term insurance, but not all contracts are renewable on a basis which makes them acceptable as long-range permanent insurance.

In most cases, you would be well advised to consider only term insurance which is renewable, and renewable by you at your sole option without evidence of insurability—that is, without submitting to a medical examination or offering other proof of your continued good health, morals, or financial standing. This privilege of renewal is of the utmost importance in any program of term insurance undertaken to cover the whole productive period of life.

When you buy renewable term insurance, you undergo a medical examination only once—when you submit your application. When the policy is about to expire, whether it is one-year, five-year, ten-year, or twenty-year term, it can be renewed.

All companies set a limit, after which no further renewals are possible. This maximum age differs, running as high as seventy-five in one case and as low as fifty-five in others. We might consider as adequate only those policies which can be renewed at least up to age sixty-five, which means that any renewal after age sixty is only for the years remaining to sixty-five. Most renewable term policies, however, do not contain this limitation and, when renewed, will run the full length of their term, even past age sixty-five. Thus, your five-year term policy renewed at age sixty-two would remain in force until you are sixty-seven; if you renewed it at age sixty-three, it would expire when you are sixty-eight, and so forth.

Periodically, a company, usually a relative newcomer to the field, announces an annual term policy which is renewable throughout life. Such companies are usually small and licensed only in a few states, so this most flexible of policies is not generally available.

Policy conversion right

In cases where life insurance is required at more advanced ages, you can exercise the right, provided by many term policies, to convert to permanent insurance without evidence of insurability. Thus, if you buy a five-year renewable and convertible term policy at age thirty-three, you could renew it as term insurance at age thirty-eight, forty-three, forty-eight, fifty-three, fifty-eight, and sixty-three. Prior to attaining age sixty-five, you can convert the policy to whole life (or any other higher-premium form) without evidence of insurability. You can carry this policy until you are 100 years of age, when most policies mature as endowments.

One should not assume however that all term insurance is renewable to age sixty-five and convertible as well. It is extremely important to check these features in any term policy you may be considering because there are policies which limit the number of renewals, such as annual term which may be renewed no more than nine times and five-year term which cannot be renewed beyond age fifty-five or sixty.

Except when the insurance is being purchased for a specific purpose and is intended to terminate after a few years, you should choose only policies which grant the option to renew until the anniversary of the policy prior to your sixty-fifth birthday. Even if you are reasonably certain that the purpose for which you are buying insurance will terminate long before then, it is advisable to enter only into contracts which give you the option to renew until this relatively advanced age. For this option may prove extremely valuable if your situation changes and you have become uninsurable in the interim.

A final caveat is in order. The policy should also be convertible up to age sixty-five to whole-life insurance. You cannot assume that a policy which is renewable to that age is necessarily also convertible. Companies often permit renewal to age sixty-five but limit convertibility to age sixty. This may

not seem important when you are buying the policy at age
thirty-five or forty, but when you reach sixty, you will need
to decide on converting to whole life if you wish to carry your
protection past age sixty-five.

Check for renewability

Checking for renewability is quite simple. Ask the agent to
show you the policy form. Policies which are not renewable,
even when they are convertible, are usually required to state
quite explicitly that they are "nonrenewable." This legend
will be found on the face of the policy or at the bottom of the
contract's first page where the broad outlines of the policy
provisions are spelled out. The renewable policy, by contrast,
is identified by a statement which indicates that it is "renewable to age _____."

The privilege of renewal will also appear in the finer print,
where it will read something like this: "This policy will be
automatically renewable at the end of _____ years from the
date of issue at the premium applicable to the insured's then
attained age according to the table below *without evidence of
insurability,* provided, however, that the insured has not attained the age of _____. It may be renewed for successive periods of _____ years until the anniversary of the policy prior
to the insured's _____ birthday." There are variations of
this phrasing according to the different companies, but all
renewable policies contain the words "may be renewed" or
"will be renewed *without evidence of insurability*" until some
stated age. A brief examination will enable you to separate
the renewable policy from one that is only convertible. If you
are in doubt after checking the contract, ask the company for
a statement in writing.

In addition to term insurance written for short periods,
many companies offer a term-to-sixty-five policy. As the name
implies, this policy may be carried until age sixty-five without
the need to renew it periodically. Other companies offer similar insurance under term expectancy, life expectancy, or some
other form which extends it to an advanced age. In the case of
these policies, the exact age at which the insurance expires
varies with the age at which the policy is issued, but in all
cases it extends through the productive period of life. All of

these policies would fulfill the requirement of "permanency."

Even though these policies are written on a low-premium basis and do not accumulate large reserves, they are designed to maintain a level premium until an advanced expiration age and are issued at premiums substantially higher than comparable term insurance written for shorter periods. Thus, whereas a five-year renewable term policy issued at age thirty-five costs $59.50 annually for $10,000, the term-to-sixty-five issued by the same company costs $121.

However, the term-to-sixty-five policy will not increase in premium as does the five-year term policy, which will be renewed at a higher premium every five years, or the one-year renewable term policy, which calls for a higher premium each year. The long-term policy eventually will be overtaken in premium cost by the shorter-period contract, which increases in cost at each renewal period. But until that point you will be paying more under the term-to-sixty-five policy than is required by the actual cost of protection at the earlier ages, and to this degree you will defeat some of the value of buying protection at the lowest possible cost. It is for this reason that you might focus on five- or ten-year renewable term.

The factor of interest on premiums should be taken into account. Would it be better to pay a larger initial premium to a dividend-paying company and anticipate premium refunds to reduce your "net cost" below that of a "guaranteed cost" company requiring a low initial premium? The policy size affects cost figures, as does the age at which a policy is issued.

Other sources of insurance

As mentioned earlier, persons who live or work in Massachusetts, New York, or Connecticut have available to them five-year renewable term insurance from mutual savings banks which is low in cost. Residents of these states, or individuals who work within their borders, will do well to compare these bank rates with those offered by life insurance companies.

Life insurance is offered by many fraternal orders. For the most part, these associations make available to their members a fairly attractive low-cost term policy; in many instances, as one of a portfolio of contracts. If you are a member of one or more of these associations, you could find it worthwhile to check their policy forms and rates.

These fraternal orders are sometimes the only life insurance carriers which offer low-cost term protection to workers in certain occupations who are refused term insurance by regular life insurance companies. For such workers, as well as for the general public, it is important to consider the usually economical and cooperatively managed life insurance offered by the fraternals. In this connection it is interesting to note that some of the fraternals have been in the life insurance business for over a hundred years and that fraternal life insurance in force today has reached the significant total of over $26 billion.

Other valuable insurance may be available from companies which cover certain occupations or professions, such as the Teachers Insurance and Annuity Association, the Presbyterian Ministers Fund, and similar organizations. If your work makes you eligible for special life insurance of this kind, you should check these policies against those of regular commercial companies.

"Minimum deposit" insurance

There is an unusual and complicated form of cash-value insurance known as "minimum deposit." It is unusual because, operating within the framework of a whole-life policy, par or nonpar, it achieves the effect of term insurance and thus might be said to incorporate the advantages of both types of coverage within a single policy—namely, the low-cost feature of term and the permanent feature of cash-value insurance.

However, the technique of converting permanent insurance to something resembling term without being limited to age sixty-five is an extremely complicated one, and it can hardly be undertaken without legal and tax counsel.

The conversion is achieved by "stripping" a whole-life policy of its cash values. This, in effect, reduces the policy to one without cash value—a characteristic of term insurance. All the available cash values in the policy are borrowed to pay the annual premium, thereby reducing the cost of the insurance to a level comparable to that of term insurance. Interest, of course, must be paid on the money which is borrowed (5 or 6 percent, depending on the state), and this expense can be covered at least in part by the annual dividend earned by the policy, in the case of a participating policy.

In event of death, the beneficiary normally would receive the face value of the policy, less the amount of loans which had been drawn against it. To prevent this erosion of face-value protection, the policyholder is permitted to buy annual increments of one-year term insurance equal to the amount of the outstanding loans. Then, in event of the policyholder's death, the beneficiary receives the face value of the whole-life policy but that amount, instead of coming entirely from the whole-life policy, comes from the insurance left in the policy (after it has been "stripped" of its cash values) plus the full amount of the term insurance.

The technique of minimum deposit proved attractive to those in high income brackets who were able to deduct the interest costs on their income tax returns, thereby in effect reducing the net cost of the insurance to the owner. Eventually, the Internal Revenue Service put something of a damper on this procedure by ruling that any four of the first seven premium payments would have to be paid entirely by the policyholder without borrowing against the cash values. If four of the first seven payments were not paid in this way, the policyholder would be ineligible to deduct from his income taxes any of the interest charges in connection with the policy.

The plan is still being sold widely, both with and without application of the tax deduction feature. Even without benefit of tax deduction, some agents claim that the minimum deposit plan, in some circumstances, can be less expensive than term insurance. The total outlay tends to fluctuate widely over the years. One minimum deposit plan, issued to a man at age thirty-five, shows total annual outlay as follows for a policy with a face value of $100,000:

Year	Total Annual Outlay
1	$1,615
2	359
3	379
4	390
5	697

The annual outlay under this particular plan fluctuates less widely over the next eight years, but beginning with the fourteenth year, when it is $817, it increases each year until it reaches $1,278 in the twentieth year. At the end of twenty years, the annual net cost of the policy averages out at $704, assuming the current dividend scale is maintained.

As compared with this figure, the same company offers a male age thirty-five $100,000 of five-year renewable term for a gross premium (before dividends) of $500, renewable at age forty for $662 annually. Thus the outlay under the term policy is less in each of the first ten years than under the minimum deposit approach.

The advisability of considering minimum deposit depends on several factors. First, the amount of benefit you derive from being able to deduct interest (this relates to your tax bracket). Second, reasonable certainty that you will remain in that bracket (or a higher one) over the course of a long period of time. Third and above all, whether you are comparing out-of-pocket costs correctly after taking into account the earning power of the extra sums you will be called on to lay out.

When all these factors have been weighed, you should check to be sure you are making a comparison with a relatively low-cost term policy. Only then will you be in a position to form a considered judgment.

CHAPTER 5

Group
Life
Insurance

In group life insurance it is fairly easy to recognize the main features of term insurance—low premiums based solely on the hazard of mortality, without accumulation of savings or retirement values.

In recent years some group plans have been instituted which are based on plans other than term insurance, but these make up only a very small percentage of the group insurance in force. With only isolated exceptions, the $630 billion of group life (representing 39 percent of the total life insurance in force in the country) is one-year term insurance.

If we compare the insurance of the usual group plan with renewable term insurance, we find that the group coverage is actually superior in several important essentials. For many workers, group insurance is very desirable. There are, however, certain limitations inherent in group insurance which seriously curtail its value for certain other workers. An outline of the pros and cons of this type of insurance will help you understand whether group life insurance has a place in your individual situation.

One of the most valuable features of group life insurance is that it makes low-cost insurance available to workers barred from insurance for any reason.

In almost every case, the charge to the insured for group insurance is substantially lower than term insurance would be, even if such term insurance were available to the worker in the particular occupation. The savings in premium to the worker, which arise in large part from the contribution made to the plan by the employer as well as from economies in mass selling, are usually quite sizable, particularly for the older employee.

While group life is actually written on a one-year term basis and has advantages in cost over most term policies, it cannot be equated with renewable term insurance in one important respect. As we saw in our study of term insurance, any long-range program to cover the productive period of life must comprise insurance which is renewable at your option until at least age sixty-five. Any plan which is limited in renewals may find you unable to continue your insurance on the term plan for as long as your insurance need exists.

If your employment is terminated

It is true your group policy may be maintained on the term basis as long as you are employed in your current job. But when your job ends, your group insurance usually ends with it. All that you can do is convert within thirty-one days to any plan except term insurance. This privilege of converting may be of benefit under certain conditions, as when you have become uninsurable in the interim. But it is obvious that if you are unemployed, you may find it difficult to pay the higher premiums required by the plan to which you have to convert if you wish to continue your insurance.

Thus, if you are insured for $10,000 under a group policy and you lose your job, the cheapest insurance to which you could convert would be whole life. Your premium for the $10,000 of insurance, if you are forty years old, will rise

Group Life Insurance Coverage

Group protection, mostly term, amounted to 42 percent of all life insurance coverage in the United States at the end of 1975.

| | | (000 omitted) | |
Year	No. of Master Policies	No. of Certificates	Amount
1915	*	120	$ 100,000
1920	6	1,600	1,570,000
1925	12	3,200	4,247,000
1930	19	5,800	9,801,000
1935	18	6,400	10,208,000
1940	23	8,800	14,938,000
1945	31	11,500	22,172,000
1950	56	19,288	47,793,000
1955	89	31,649	101,345,000
1960	169	43,602	175,903,000
1961	180	46,262	192,794,000
1962	193	48,568	209,950,000
1963	203	51,062	229,477,000
1964	219	54,695	253,620,000
1965	234	60,930	308,078,000
1966	249	64,594	345,945,000
1967	261	68,818	394,501,000
1968	275	72,895	442,778,000
1969	290	75,527	488,864,000
1970	304	79,844	551,357,000
1971	312	82,320	589,883,000
1972	326	85,102	640,689,000
1973	338	88,385	708,322,000
1974	359	93,567	827,018,000
1975	378	96,693	904,695,000

*Fewer than 50 policies.

Sources: *Spectator Year Book*, Institute of Life Insurance

rather sharply—from about $72 a year to about $230.50 in a nonparticipating company, or to $290 in a participating policy. By contrast, if you had been insured under an individual term policy, your premium at this age would be about $81.10, which you might be better able to meet despite your loss of employment.

The increase will be even more dramatic if you are older when your employment terminates. The group rate you have been paying is usually the same regardless of your age but the whole-life policy to which you will convert will reflect the higher age. Thus, if you are fifty, a nonparticipating whole-life policy will call for an annual premium of some $350; if participating, it will be over $400 per annum.

Group insurance cannot therefore be equated with renewable term insurance, for the latter can be carried throughout the productive period of life.

The group policy offers low-cost protection as long as you remain in the "insured" job. At the termination of your present employment, you may find an insured group in your new job, in which case you can continue your group insurance at the advantageously low group rate. In any event, if your new work has no group coverage, you can buy individual whole-life insurance, which is as cheap as any protection you can get at that time. Until that date, you have the advantage of the lower rates of group protection.

The problem will not prove as severe if you have not become uninsurable. You could then arrange to replace the group insurance you are being forced to give up with a renewable term policy. While the group protection is cheaper than individual term insurance, renewable term insurance has the important advantage that you can maintain your insurance as long as you need it and can pay the premiums, whether or not you continue on your present job.

Improvement in group insurance

A developing tendency in group insurance which promises to do away with some of the nonpermanence of this form of coverage should be noted. Labor unions have become increasingly interested in group insurance and many are administering such insurance plans directly or in conjunction with employers in their industries. Under many of these plans, particularly those administered by a union, the worker can continue his insurance on the low-rate basis not only while he is employed but also during slack seasons and layoffs if he maintains his membership in the union. Group insurance treated in this fashion is easily superior in permanence to plans which require uninterrupted employment for the continuance of the insurance.

Even when you are not barred from buying individual insurance, you should join the insured group where you work. If, in common with many other wage earners, you cannot afford a life insurance estate as large as you would like, the group policy offers a comparatively painless way to increase your life insurance without too much increase in premium outlay. This low-cost protection will be yours at least throughout the duration of your employment on your insured job.

CHAPTER 6

Changing Insurance Policies

If you are at present carrying life insurance and find that the policies do not meet your requirements, you may wish to replace them. Such a changeover would appear to be proper, provided certain precautions are kept in mind.

In checking your life insurance and the policies on members of your family, you will find it most efficient to proceed as though you were buying insurance for the first time. The initial step in arriving at a life insurance program, you will recall, was to determine your need for life insurance, and the size of this need. If you follow the technique outlined in Chapter 2 for estimating life insurance requirements, you may find that some members of your family are carrying life insurance which is not warranted by a real need of protection against the hazards of "economic death."

A large part of the insurance sold on the lives of children

falls into this group of unnecessary life insurance. As we have seen, life insurance is not the equivalent of regular savings, nor can insurance justifiably be urged on young lives merely because it will give the insured a later advantage in "lower rates." Except where insurance is calculated to provide a "burial" fund, there seems little justification for juvenile insurance.

We have seen that insurance is an unnecessary expense when maintained on adult lives which do not require protection against economic death. Maintaining more than a small amount of insurance to provide a "clean-up fund" is therefore unwarranted on the lives of single persons without financial responsibilities, or on old people already past their productive period, as it is for anyone whose death would not cause a financial loss to dependents.

An exception to this rule might exist to a degree in the case of some mothers. Though a mother may make no actual monetary contribution to the family treasury, the loss of her services might place an extra economic burden on the father. This risk of such loss might properly be covered by some life insurance.

When to discontinue a policy

Insurance you or your family may be carrying which does not measure up to these standards of life insurance requirements might be reexamined with a view to possibly dropping it.

Some insurance companies allow what is known as a midperiod surrender. This returns a cash value plus a pro rata premium refund to the policyholder for the unexpired part of the premium payment period. The policy is then terminated. If your insurance company does not permit a mid-period surrender, you can ask for the maximum loan value on your policy, where such loan value exists. At the end of the policy year, you will receive a notice of premium due which will include a charge for interest on the loan. At this point, you can inform the company that you wish to discontinue your policy and to receive in cash any equity remaining in the policy, as well as dividends which may have accrued.

Depending on how old your policy is and on the amount of

its cash value, it is often advisable to keep the policy in force by borrowing from the policy each year to pay the premium due. As the interest charges will mount annually, it will not be wise to follow this procedure indefinitely.

Dropping insurance on lives which have no need for protection will often make it possible to increase the insurance where it does belong—on the life of the person who makes a financial contribution to the support of others.

Life insurance on children and other nonproductive lives depends on the earnings of the head of the family. If death should remove this source of support, payments for insurance on the lives of the dependents would be seriously jeopardized. Furthermore, if this insurance had been maintained at the expense of adequate protection on the breadwinner's life, the consequences could be most serious.

If you want a new policy

If you find, after analysis of your estate requirements, that you require life insurance protection, the question of how to change to renewable term insurance may arise.

It is obvious that your insurance conversion program will depend on your present insurability. If you have developed some medical, moral, or financial impairment since you last purchased life insurance, there may not be much you can do except to hold on to your present life insurance estate.

There is only one sure way to check on your present insurability and that is to apply for the actual term insurance you wish to buy. When the policy is issued and you have paid the first premium, you are in a position to discontinue your higher-premium policies.

Disadvantages of replacing policies

Several important points can be made against replacing policies. For one, your old policy, if it is two years old, is now "incontestable," and the new policy will not attain this status until you have kept it in force for two years from the date of issue. Prior to that time, your new policy may be canceled by the company if it can prove that you obtained it by fraud or by concealing some fact which is material to the acceptance of the risk. After a period of two years during which you have

Life Expectancy in the United States

Age	WHITE Male	Female	ALL OTHER Male	Female	TOTAL Male	Female
			(years)			
0	68.9	76.6	62.9	71.2	68.2	75.9
20	51.0	58.1	45.7	53.5	50.4	57.5
40	32.6	38.9	29.3	35.3	32.2	38.5
45	28.1	34.3	25.5	31.1	27.9	33.9
50	24.0	29.8	22.0	27.1	23.8	29.5
55	20.1	25.5	18.7	23.4	19.9	25.3
60	16.5	21.4	16.0	19.9	16.5	21.3
65	13.4	17.6	13.4	16.7	13.4	17.5
70	10.6	14.0	11.1	13.7	10.7	13.9

Note: Figures are for 1974.

Sources: U.S. Department of Health, Education, and Welfare, Institute of Life Insurance

kept the new policy in force, it too becomes incontestable.

While the "incontestability" clause is an important protection for policyholders, and its inclusion represented a great step forward in removing the threat of court action from most death claims, it offers no reason to deter you from rewriting your present policy, if you can answer the questions on the application truthfully.

Also, most new policies carry a "suicide" clause which releases the company from liability in case of suicide within the first two years. In your present policy, if it is more than two years old, suicide most likely is covered.

Disability income provision

A more important omission from your new policy would be the loss of a disability income provision that might now be irreplaceable, particularly if you have been carrying your policy for a long time. Many old policies offered a provision under which the insured would receive a monthly income in the event he became totally and permanently disabled. Disability income provisions varied considerably. There were differences not only between companies but often in the same company due to revisions made throughout the years.

One important variation, for example, provided that each monthly payment to the insured would decrease the amount of life insurance payable at death. Other differences involved the amount of monthly income payable for each $1,000 of insurance, the period during which the insured must be continuously disabled before beginning to receive his monthly income, the maximum age covered by the clause, and the definition of total and permanent disability.

There are other more subtle differences which may not become apparent to you except in special circumstances. For our purpose, it is sufficient to be aware of the possible variations in life insurance disability income clauses.

If your present insurance provides for monthly income disability benefits, you must take this feature into account before discontinuing your policy. In some cases, you may be able to buy term insurance with the disability income provision, although this is not commonly offered. Even when such disability income benefits are available as an added feature, the older disability clause may well be substantially more liberal. Present-day clauses are usually more circumscribed than many older disability clauses, so a careful comparison must be made. Check with your insurance agent or the company about this point.

Other disability coverage

In considering this aspect, you should know that there are noncancelable accident and health policies which compare favorably with the disability clauses in life insurance policies. This type of policy is taken up in the section of this book devoted to accident and health insurance. While many of these

Ordinary Life Insurance Policyholder Deaths by Cause, 1975

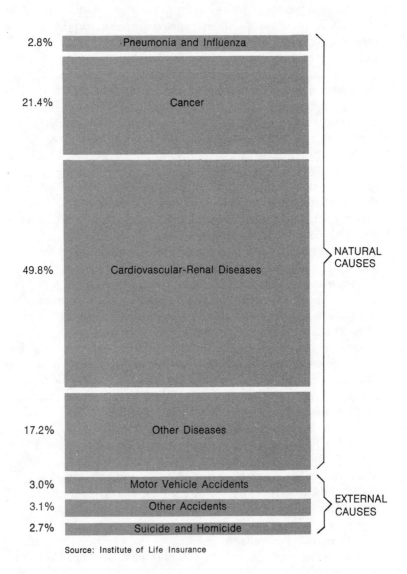

2.8%	Pneumonia and Influenza	
21.4%	Cancer	NATURAL CAUSES
49.8%	Cardiovascular-Renal Diseases	
17.2%	Other Diseases	
3.0%	Motor Vehicle Accidents	
3.1%	Other Accidents	EXTERNAL CAUSES
2.7%	Suicide and Homicide	

Source: Institute of Life Insurance

contracts may be found to be more expensive than the extra premiums charged for disability coverage in the life insurance policy, there are advantages in having a life insurance estate separated from a disability or health program, as will be shown in a later chapter.

Furthermore, in comparing costs, it is important to be aware of the fact that the extra premium you pay each year for disability is not necessarily the only charge made for this feature. If your present life insurance contains a disability income provision, you may be paying an "unseen" charge each year for this protection. This extra charge for disability above the one stated in the policy arises from the practice of some companies to draw up a separate dividend scale for policies containing the disability clause. In such cases, the dividends of a policy containing the disability clause are much lower than those of policies without the disability provision.

The extra premium for disability shown in such policies is thus really only a fraction of the real cost of this feature. You may own a policy which shows an additional premium of $20 for the disability provision on $10,000 of insurance, but you may actually be paying two or three times as much if you were able to compute the dividends lost to you each year because your policy contains the disability clause.

The provision for monthly income in event of total and permanent disability which we have been considering should not be confused with disability clauses which allow merely for waiver of premiums. The latter feature, which is available from almost every life insurance company, provides that your policy will be continued in force without further premium payments in the event you are totally and permanently disabled.

There are other objections to replacing your policy. For example, a proposed new participating policy may not pay dividends for the first year or two. Also, dropping a policy within certain years may involve a "surrender charge" to cover the company's cost in handling your policy—commissions, salaries, and so forth.

Complication in replacing policy

No insurance which you need should be terminated before

you have replaced it with a new policy. This necessary pre-caution produces a complication. Many companies ask in their life insurance application whether the insurance you are ap-plying for "is intended to replace any policy or policies in this or any other company," or some similarly phrased question. If this question is answered in the affirmative, the company may hold up the issuance of the new policy for two weeks and notify your present company in order to give it an opportu-nity to discuss with you the advisability of making the change. This procedure, subscribed to by most of the larger companies in the United States and Canada, is known as "A Plan for Discouraging the Replacement of Life Insurance of One Company by New Insurance in Another Company."

In an effort to discourage replacement, most states now re-quire that any proposal to a client recommending replace-ment of an old policy be made in writing and that it set forth all the pros and cons of the suggested changeover. Many stat-utes require that a copy of this proposal be kept on file at the company's home office for a stated number of years.

There is, however, nothing in the existing laws of any state to prohibit one insurance company from replacing the policy of another company, except where misrepresentation or omis-sion to state a material fact is used in selling the new policy.

The following instruction from the Prudential Insurance Company's rate book seems to be typical of the attitude pre-vailing in most companies: "The agent must be sure that no previous insurance is given up at a sacrifice."

In determining this point, you and your agent must take due account of the fact that a new policy incurs "front load" costs which you already have paid under your old policy and that abandonment of an old policy may mean the loss of such valuable features as the incontestability clause for a period of two years and possibly of disability income provisions.

Another, more recent development to consider is the in-crease to 8 percent from 6 percent in the interest on policy loans. This change has been authorized by thirty-four states, and a number of the leading companies have adopted this rate. It will not affect the purchaser of a term insurance policy, which does not develop cash or loan values. It could, however, enter into a consideration of the purchase of life insurance plans, such as the minimum deposit plan, which are based on borrowing heavily against accumulated cash values so as to hold premium payments to a minimum.

CHAPTER 7

Questions
and
Answers

Insurance companies, as you may know, will accept premium payments either annually, semiannually, quarterly, or, in many cases, even on a monthly basis. However, you should be aware that the most economical practice is to pay all premiums annually. The extra charges for deferring payments vary, but even in the case of the more advantageous companies you will save by paying your premiums once a year.

What does it cost to defer premiums?

Generally the extra charge when paying on a semiannual basis amounts to about 8 percent. On a quarterly basis, the charge is about 11 percent. Monthly premiums involve an even higher charge. These extra charges cover interest and also the additional costs of collection, the nondeduction of deferred premiums at death, and the loss of interest earnings to the insurance company as compared to premiums paid annually.

If you have difficulty in meeting the full annual premium in a single payment, deferred plans can be helpful. Nevertheless, if you are paying premiums more frequently than once a year—fractionally, as it is called—you might consider the possibility of saving money by borrowing the additional sums you need from the insurance company to pay the annual premium. It would not be wise to do this unless you set up and follow a plan to repay the loan as regularly as you are now paying the premiums. And this method is not really worth all the trouble involved unless you are dealing with premiums of sizable amounts.

What option should you select for dividends?

If you are insured in a mutual company or under any participating policy—some three-fifths of the insurance in force is of this kind—you will usually receive notice of dividends apportioned to your policy for the year. Such notice is generally made on the bill the company sends you for the following year's premium. Most companies begin to pay dividends ("refunds") at the end of the second or third year, although a few pay a first-year dividend.

You may apply the dividend towards the premium payment that is due, or you may elect to pay the gross premium and leave the dividend to accumulate at interest. Before deciding to leave the dividend to accumulate at interest, you should find out how the interest rate paid by the insurance company compares with that available from other thrift institutions.

Another possibility is to use the dividend to purchase paid-up additional insurance without a medical examination. Additional amounts of insurance offered under this option are charged at "net rates," that is, without any "loading" to take care of company expenses, but the form of insurance is single-premium life insurance, which calls for a very high one-time outlay per $1,000 of insurance. If you are uninsurable and if you want to increase the amount of protection for your family, this option will answer an important need. Otherwise, you may do better to take the dividend in cash and put it to work at a higher rate of interest.

In some companies, under certain policies, still another option is offered—the purchase, without a physical examination, of one-year term additions up to the amount of the cash value. If you need additional insurance, this is an economical way to add to your estate.

In any event, you should check all your participating policies to determine what disposition is being made of the dividends. Too often, these are accumulated at a low rate of interest without an awareness on the part of the policyholder that he might secure higher earnings for his dividends by depositing them elsewhere.

Should you name a beneficiary?

Naming a specific beneficiary or beneficiaries will give your policy several advantages over those made payable simply to "the estate of the insured." First, it may avoid the complications and expense of drawn-out probate or administration proceedings in the courts concerning the proceeds of your life insurance. Second, in certain states, policies made payable to a named beneficiary, and more particularly to a wife, are free from actions on the part of the insured's creditors and, in some cases, from actions of the beneficiary's creditors. Third, state tax advantages may result if insurance money is left to a named beneficiary.

Should you name a contingent beneficiary?

It is advisable to name a contingent beneficiary in addition to the first beneficiary. A contingent beneficiary becomes entitled to the insurance money only if the primary beneficiary is not alive when the policy becomes payable. If the beneficiary named in your policy dies and you do not substitute a new beneficiary, at your death your insurance would be payable to your estate, resulting in expense and complications.

A contingent beneficiary can be named when you buy your policy or may be incorporated into your present insurance. In your application for insurance or for beneficiary clause alteration, you need specify only that your insurance be paid "to _____, if living; if not living, to _____."

If you make your policy payable under one of the installment options which will be discussed later, you should designate additional beneficiaries besides the primary one. For, in the event that your primary beneficiary did not survive to receive all the installments which are payable or guaranteed and you had not named any other person as additional beneficiary, any unpaid installments would be paid to your beneficiary's estate.

To see how this works, let us assume you direct that your $25,000 policy be paid to your wife in monthly installments of $250 until exhausted. The insurance money will last for ten years (in a company crediting 4 percent interest on policy proceeds left with it). If your wife begins to receive monthly payments at your death but does not live to exhaust the principal, the balance of the monthly installments will be paid to her estate.

This may be acceptable, especially if you have children born of the marriage and her will has made provisions for them. If, on the other hand, you want to name the person or persons to receive any unpaid balance at her death, you should designate the contingent beneficiary/ies.

It is important that you discuss with your attorney the courses open to you before making a decision in this matter.

What is the "common disaster" clause?

The mounting death toll of automobile and aircraft accidents in recent years has included an increased number of married couples. In such a double accident, if the beneficiary wife survives the husband, if only by a few hours, his insurance becomes payable to her estate, even if the policy named a contingent beneficiary.

The contingent beneficiary clause becomes operative only if the primary beneficiary is not living at the insured's death. Since the wife in this case was living at the insured's death, she was entitled to the proceeds of her husband's insurance. At her death, regardless of when it takes place, the proceeds are paid to her estate. If there are no children, the insurance money might in this way be paid to persons for whom you have no intention of providing at your death.

If there are children of the marriage, they will be in line to receive the proceeds which their mother did not live to spend, unless her will directs otherwise. But the proceeds will require probate or administrative action, with the consequent expenses of such procedure. Furthermore, the proceeds of the policy may be subject to claims by the wife's creditors.

To meet the contingency of a "common disaster," many beneficiary clauses are now drawn as follows: ". . . to the insured's wife, _____, if living at the expiration of *seven days* after the death of the insured; if not then living, in equal shares to such of the insured's children as shall then be living . . ."

It is permissible to name additional contingent beneficiaries to receive proceeds of insurance policies in the event that the first contingent beneficiary does not survive the insured. Thus the "common disaster" clause just quoted might be augmented to read as follows: ". . . to the insured's wife, _____, if living at the expiration of *seven days* after the death of the insured; if not then living, in equal shares to such of the insured's children as shall then be living; should none then be living, to the insured's mother, if then living . . ."

Should your insurance be paid in a lump sum?

Whether to have all or part of your insurance paid in a lump sum at your death should be decided only after you have carefully considered your individual situation, including the value of your liquid assets, the number of your dependents and their ages, and the special needs of your family members. Also to be taken into account are the benefits to which your dependents may be entitled under Social Security.

Arranging to have your insurance paid in installments has advantages. It avoids the danger that your beneficiary, who may be inexperienced in business matters, might dissipate these important funds in unwise investment or speculation. Also, in most states, payments from life insurance proceeds being received by a beneficiary are not subject to creditors' claims or attachments.

Arranging your insurance under an optional mode of settlement, as installment payments are called, will give you reasonable assurance that the provisions you have made for your family's basic needs will be available as you directed. It should be understood, however, that directing the insurance company to pay your insurance in installments will sacrifice the important element of flexibility. Your family's circumstances

Life Insurance Benefit Payments

Americans received $22.5 billion in payments from life insurance policies and annuities in 1975.

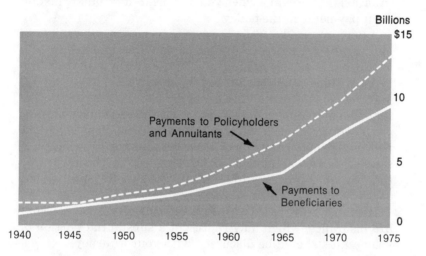

Source: Institute of Life Insurance

years after you are gone cannot be foreseen. Emergencies may arise; inflation may make an income which is adequate today totally inadequate with the passage of years; and profitable opportunities for investment may open to your heirs.

It is necessary to remember that the insurance company cannot exercise discretionary powers; it must follow your instructions to the letter regardless of the problems that arise to plague your beneficiaries.

All too often, an insurance policy is earmarked for the college education of a child when the wife, if she were suddenly widowed, would have great difficulty getting the youngster through high school.

If you, the insured, make no special provisions, some flexibility will be possible for your beneficiary. When policy proceeds are payable in a single sum, the beneficiary can elect to leave all or part of the money with the insurance company to be paid under any of the settlement options in the contract. When the beneficiary makes such arrangements, she retains the right to withdraw the funds at any time, in contrast to the situation that prevails when you, the insured, stipulate installment payments in the policy.

A compromise between the two extremes may be achieved by providing that the insurance be paid in stipulated installments, but with the right of the beneficiary to withdraw limited additional sums within any calendar year.

If you should feel it important that the administration of funds for your dependents include more discretionary powers, you could arrange a life insurance trust under which the policies are made payable to a trustee for your beneficiary. A separate trust agreement can be drawn up by you regarding the insurance proceeds to be received by the trustee at your death.

It cannot be stressed too often that the disposition of your life insurance, which may represent a substantial portion of your estate, should be discussed with your attorney.

PART TWO

Coverage for Accidents and Illness

CHAPTER 8

Your
Disability
Insurance

One of the most serious economic hazards of modern life is the threat of a disabling injury or illness.

Even a relatively brief period of incapacity may bring with it fairly serious economic disruption because most disability is double-edged in effect. It cuts off the income of the wage earner at the very time when he must assume a burden of medical expenses.

A disability that is protracted may prove economically shattering. Any reserves that may have been accumulated are quickly exhausted, and the disabled person becomes entangled in serious debt or must turn to some form of charity.

There is no question that provision against the more drastic consequences of disability fills a real need in the lives of the great majority of people who depend on regular, gainful work for their own support and the maintenance of their families.

Such protection against the financial distress of illness or injury should compensate not only for the loss of earnings during a disability but also for some of the expenses of medical, hospital, and surgical care.

Protection for employees

The Workmen's Compensation statutes in effect in every state provide some measure of protection for the economic consequences of work-connected injuries and .disabilities. Even when a disability does not arise out of and in the course of employment, many industries have taken steps to provide for the continuance, at least during temporary periods of incapacity, of a worker's wages or some portion of his regular earnings.

A number of days of sick leave may be stipulated in the agreement between the employer and his employees, or some form of health insurance provided, for which the employer pays all or a large part of the costs. Even where no definite arrangements have been entered into, an employee can often look forward to receiving his salary at least during brief periods of illness or injury.

In addition, a growing number of employee benefit associations, farm groups, fraternal societies, and various other voluntary organizations are taking steps to provide some protection for their members against the economic consequences of disability. Many communities are now encouraging or sponsoring some form of medical and hospital coverage for their residents. On all sides, there is a growing recognition of the economic dislocation of disability, and steps are being taken to budget for these contingencies.

Five states (California, Hawaii, New Jersey, New York, and Rhode Island) and Puerto Rico have made it mandatory for employers to provide protection against temporary disabilities which are not related to the work activities of the employee. The larger portion of the premium for this coverage is borne by the employer. While the provisions differ among these states, they all cover the loss of wages for a stipulated number of weeks, usually twenty-six in a calendar year.

At the other end of the disability spectrum is the protection afforded under Social Security for long-term disabilities.

Estimating your requirements

Any such protection as is available to you on a group basis, as well as the coverage under government or state-sponsored disability programs, must be taken into account in estimating your personal requirements for disability insurance. Even where such group protection is provided, many wage earners will find that a disabling injury or illness of extended duration would be almost certain to cause severe hardship. For such people, some additional protection in the form of personal accident, health, and medical insurance would seem advisable. However, the cost of such insurance is relatively high.

The extent of your need for insurance against loss of time due to disability will depend on your individual situation. Your employer may provide for some definite sick leave each year, or you may be able to count on receiving your salary, or some part of it, during periods of incapacity. If you run your own business, your income may continue, even if on a curtailed basis, during less protracted illness or accidental injury. If you derive any support from investments, property, commissions, or royalties, such income may continue despite your temporary withdrawal from active work.

Naturally, in any consideration of your need for disability protection, the question of your family situation will play a large part. The number of your dependents, the household expenses that must continue, the emergency adjustments that may be possible, the help you can count on from others in the family—all these factors will determine how long you can meet a disability without undue hardship. Equally important is the amount of savings or other reserves you can call on in an emergency. An estimate of these factors will provide a working basis for assessing the extent of your need for insurance against loss of time through a disabling injury or illness.

Group insurance eligibility

An important place in your disability program may be filled by insurance for which you are eligible as a member of a group. Several types of insurance of this kind may be open to you. First, there is the group accident and sickness insurance available to most employees of well-established companies. The benefits under this type of coverage are usually restricted to a limited number of weeks in any one year or for any continuous disability.

The cost to the insured worker for this form of protection is usually quite low because of the contributions the employer makes to the upkeep of the plan and certain economies inherent in this type of underwriting. In some cases, the employer pays the entire premium for this insurance. These plans have the further advantage of bringing accident and health insurance to workers who might otherwise be ineligible for such protection because of their medical history. Any worker in an insured firm may join the group without giving evidence of his insurability, even if he has previously been rejected for an individual accident and health policy. It is usually stipulated that all employees must come into the insured group within thirty-one days after they become eligible for the insurance. After this time, the insurance company has the right to ask for a medical examination, and is free to reject any applicant.

While such plans, like all group insurance, terminate after you leave a particular firm, they do offer protection against temporary incapacities while you are on the payroll and in some cases during periods of layoff. Despite the limitation on the permanence of this insurance, most people who can come under a group disability plan at their place of employment will find this insurance advantageous.

Some workers are also covered by a group long-term disability plan which pays an income until age sixty-five even though an employee is no longer on the company payroll. Provisions for disability are also available under a few of the pension plans that are in force in certain industries. These plans provide for a reduced pension to be paid to a worker who becomes disabled and must retire before normal retirement age.

Union and industry plans

Similar in many ways to these types of group insurance is the growing field of sickness benefit programs established through collective bargaining between a trade union and an industry. These plans show considerable variation in the amount of benefits to which a worker is entitled, the period of

Work Fatalities and Injuries

Year	Total Employed (millions)	Fatalities	Fatalities per 100,000 Workers	Injuries	Injuries per 100,000 Workers
1950	58.9	15,500	26.3	1,950,000	3,211
1951	60.0	16,000	26.7	2,100,000	3,500
1952	60.3	15,000	24.9	2,000,000	3,317
1953	61.2	15,000	24.5	2,000,000	3,268
1954	60.1	14,000	23.3	1,850,000	3,078
1955	62.2	14,200	22.8	1,900,000	3,055
1956	63.8	14,300	22.4	2,000,000	3,135
1957	64.1	14,200	22.2	1,950,000	3,042
1958	63.0	13,300	21.1	1,800,000	2,857
1959	64.6	13,800	21.4	1,950,000	3,019
1960	65.8	13,800	21.0	1,950,000	2,964
1961	65.7	13,500	20.5	1,900,000	2,892
1962	66.7	13,700	20.5	2,000,000	2,999
1963	67.8	14,200	20.9	2,000,000	2,950
1964	69.3	14,200	20.5	2,050,000	2,958
1965	71.1	14,100	19.8	2,100,000	2,954
1966	72.9	14,500	19.9	2,200,000	3,018
1967	74.3	14,200	19.1	2,200,000	2,961
1968	75.9	14,300	18.8	2,200,000	2,898
1969	77.9	14,300	18.2	2,200,000	2,824
1970	78.6	13,800	17.6	2,200,000	2,798
1971	79.1	13,700	17.3	2,300,000	2,908
1972	81.7	14,000	17.1	2,400,000	2,938
1973	84.4	13,400	16.9	2,500,000	2,962
1974	85.9	13,400	15.6	2,300,000	2,678

Sources: National Safety Council, Bureau of Labor Statistics, Insurance Information Institute

disability covered, and the method of administration and financing. Most of the plans are financed entirely by the employer, but in a few cases employer and employee contribute jointly. Administration of the plan may be exclusively in the hands of the trade union, or handled jointly by the employer and the union, or entirely by a private insurance company.

Disability insurance as part of the agreement between a trade union and an employer is a fairly recent development that is growing rapidly. Certain advantages have become apparent in these plans as compared to straight group insurance. For one thing, the union or jointly administered insurance program, which is part of the contract between the employer and his employees, is not subject to discontinuance or alteration by the employer, as in the case of the straight group plan.

Also, plans established by collective bargaining endeavor to bring the entire industry into the insurance program. A worker who leaves one firm for a job in another section of the industry can usually step into an insurance plan similar to the one he left behind.

Trade union or jointly administered insurance thus offers another fairly effective plan of protection against temporary disabilities, at least during a worker's employment period.

There are also trade union accident and sickness insurance programs which are supported entirely by membership dues or assessments. These plans appear to be less numerous and important than those instituted through collective bargaining. They do, however, offer some relatively permanent protection to the insured since they can be continued for at least as long as the worker remains a member of the union.

Many fraternal orders, societies, and mutual benefit and aid associations offer their members some sickness and accident benefits. The coverage is usually circumscribed, but some protection during periods of disabling injury or illness is made available to large numbers of people who are members of such organizations.

Covering extended disability

Because long-continuing invalidism could be catastrophic in its consequences, protection against this hazard should be the first step in your accident and health insurance program.

Shorter periods of illness or injury can be met with much less difficulty.

To cover permanent or extended disability, policies are written which pay benefits only after the illness or injury has been the cause of continuous disability of a definite duration. The period excluded from the policy's coverage is usually referred to as the elimination period. Any dependable insurance that covers long-range disabilities carries a fairly extensive elimination period, as does the disability coverage under Social Security.

It is often argued that policies with long elimination periods do not provide insurance for the great majority of claims. It is true that a very high percentage of claims do not extend past a few days, but this fact must be seen in its proper light.

Without getting too involved in disability statistics, we can understand that the number of the claims is no real index to the degree of the disability hazard. Thus, you may be subject to six times as many short-term disabilities as those of longer duration. But one illness that lasts a year or five years or continues throughout life will cost you more than all the conditions that interfere with your earning power for a few days or weeks.

While figures on the economic toll from long-term disabilities can only be estimated, it is reasonably clear that the number of days lost from work is very large. Thus, "if the crude rate of occurrence of long-term disability is taken as ten per 1,000 workers exposed and the average duration of such long-term disability is assumed to be three years (after the six-month qualification period), this would indicate that in any year there are thirty workers per 1,000 disabled. . . . It would indicate an estimated income loss from long-term disability of $11 billion per year." [1]

Protection under Social Security

Before you set out on your quest for long-term disability insurance, you should understand the very valuable protec-

---

1. Dickerson, O.D., *Health Insurance*, Richard D. Irwin, Inc., Homewood, Ill. 3rd ed., 1968, pp. 17-18. The writer points out in a footnote that these figures are probably conservative, as they are based on insurance experience and insured persons are medically selected.

tion against this hazard which has been made available under Social Security.

There are several classes of persons eligible for disability benefits under the Social Security Act, e.g., persons disabled before age twenty-two who continue to be disabled, disabled widows, disabled dependent widowers, and (under certain conditions) disabled surviving divorced wives of workers who were insured at their death. But the chief beneficiaries of this coverage are disabled workers under sixty-five and their families, and it is this group's benefits which will be outlined here.

In order for a worker to be eligible, he must have been working under Social Security for certain minimum periods. The extent of the period required depends on his age at the onset of his disability, as follows:

Under age twenty-four: A worker who is disabled before he is twenty-four must have been working for at least one and a half years in the three-year period ending when his disability began.

Age twenty-four through thirty: A worker in this age group when disabled must have worked half the time in the period beginning when he was twenty-one and ending when his disability began.

Age thirty-one or older: Generally, workers in this age group need credit for at least five years out of the ten ending when the disability began. The years need not be continuous or in units of full years. There are some exceptions to this rule, and requirements are eased for blind persons.

A worker is considered disabled under the Social Security law if his physical or mental condition prevents him from doing any substantial gainful work and the condition is expected to last at least twelve months or to result in death. It is important to note that the law does not require the disability to be or appear to be permanent. Even if recovery can be expected, a worker is eligible for benefits if the condition which prevents him from engaging in gainful work is expected to last twelve months.

In addition to the disabled worker, benefits will also be paid to his family members in the following categories: unmarried children under eighteen or under twenty-two if in

full-time attendance at a school; unmarried children age
eighteen or over who were disabled before they reached
twenty-two and continue disabled; a wife of any age who has
in her care a child under eighteen or disabled who is receiving benefits based on the father's Social Security record; a
wife age sixty-two or older, regardless of whether there are
any children entitled to benefits; and, under certain circumstances, grandchildren, stepchildren, and adopted children.

No benefits are payable for the first five months of a disability. The first payment that can be received is for the sixth
month of disability. The amount of the benefits is based on the
average wages of the worker for a certain number of years
before he became disabled. While the exact amount of these
benefits cannot be figured in advance, a reasonable estimate
can be arrived at. If you are sixty years old in 1975 and have
been earning the maximum creditable earnings for Social
Security since 1951, you will become entitled to $341.70 per
month; if your wife is sixty-two, the benefit will be $469.90.
A forty-year-old disabled worker with a wife under sixty-five
and one child can receive as much as $668.80 per month.

A choice of benefits

Disability benefits are not paid in addition to other benefits
under Social Security. If you become entitled to more than one
benefit at the same time, the amount you will be paid will be
equal to the larger of the benefits. Payments to a disabled
worker are converted to retirement benefits when he becomes
eligible for such benefits.

If a worker under sixty-two whose disability arises out of
and in the course of his employment receives Workmen's
Compensation benefits, the total payments to him and his
family may not exceed 80 percent of his average monthly
wages before he became disabled.

Even if these benefits are considered as payable only to age
sixty-five (when the worker's retirement benefits would come
into play), it can be seen that they can amount to a considerable sum and can loom large in the disability protection picture. Thus, a worker who becomes eligible for a monthly benefit of $327.10 at age forty can receive nearly $100,000 in benefits by the time he is sixty-five.

Estimating your benefits

While the protection afforded by Social Security is of great importance, for many persons a serious gap may exist between the government-sponsored program and a minimum standard for maintaining themselves during protracted or permanent disabilities. Before you enter into the realm of private insurance, you should endeavor to arrive at a reasonable estimate of the disability benefits you may count on.

For information about your benefits, you may visit any office of the Social Security Administration of the Department of Health, Education, and Welfare. For an easy-to-understand booklet on the disability provisions of the law, write to the Superintendent of Documents, United States Government Printing Office, Washington, D.C. 20402. Ask for DHEW Publication No. (SSA) 73-10029 and enclose forty cents to cover its cost.

Benefits under Social Security generally being inadequate, you must find ways to add to the coverage for long-term and permanent disabling illnesses or accidents.

You should check into the salary continuance agreements or arrangements which may cover you at your place of employment and into the group insurance, if any, provided for the employees of your company. As in the case of the previously mentioned statutory disability benefits provided in five states and Puerto Rico, most of these company-sponsored plans tend to emphasize shorter-term disability protection and may therefore be disregarded in planning for more serious and extended periods of disability.

If, after you have tallied all the benefits available to you under Social Security and group and fraternal insurance, you find that you need to add to this protection package, you will do well to direct your attention to guaranteed renewable (and wherever possible noncancelable) accident and sickness policies which promise indemnity for the longer-lasting disabilities arising out of accident or illness.

CHAPTER 9

What to
Watch for

It might appear superfluous to point out that a first requirement in any insurance program is that it provide protection
when you need it. And yet many accident and health insurance
policies offer little or no guarantee of this sort, and you cannot
be certain that the disabilities or infirmities you may incur
will be covered.

Many companies are still issuing accident and health policies which are written so that their continuance in force depends entirely on the company. The most drastic clause of this
type states explicitly: "The company may cancel this policy
at any time by written notice delivered to the insured or
mailed to his last address as shown by the records of the
company."

While many states now prohibit the issuance of new policies
which can be canceled except on policy anniversaries, such

contracts are still offered in many jurisdictions, and countless policyholders who purchased their policies before these protective statutes were enacted are still carrying contracts with this condition. Under a policy with a cancellation clause of this type, the insurance company need not explain its reasons for canceling, and you have no recourse against such a decision, regardless of how long you have maintained the policy in force.

Even though your policy covering disability may not contain a specific clause giving the company the right to cancel at any time, it may be nonrenewable.

The company may retain the option of renewal at the expiration of any year or policy period. The exact phrasing of the clause covering this factor varies in different cases, and does not always appear in the same part of the policy. Often, in the early paragraphs the policy reads: "It takes effect on the ____ day of ____ and continues in effect until the ____ day of ____; it may be renewed with the consent of the company for further consecutive periods..."

This option of the company to renew or refuse to renew a policy at the end of any policy period may also appear as follows: "The insurance granted hereunder shall terminate at noon, standard time, at the place of the insured's residence, ____ day of ____, unless the policy be renewed from term to term by the payment in advance of an annual, semiannual, or quarterly premium and its acceptance by the company."

Check your policy

It is important that you check your policy to see if some such clause appears. Until fairly recently some companies would label such policies noncancelable because there was no clearcut cancellation privilege. All states now prohibit the use of the word "noncancelable" on such policies issued today, but older policies now in force may still carry this legend. It will, therefore, be best for you to check your policy even if the word noncancelable is displayed on it.

If you have any doubts about the renewable feature of a policy, be sure to ask the insurance company for a written statement that the policy is renewable at your sole option until a definite age.

The contract which states that it "may be renewed with the consent of the company for further consecutive periods" is usually written for one year. This gives the insurance company the option of deciding at the end of each year whether it cares to renew the policy. Your policy may be only one year old or may have been renewed for the past twenty years, but the company has the sole and unrestricted option at any renewal date to terminate the insurance. Again, as in the case of the cancelable policy, you have no recourse against such action. Even if your application for the policy was scrupulously accurate in all its statements, the contract is terminated and the company is not required to supply any reason for its decision.

If this should happen, you could try to obtain insurance from another company, but your chances of acceptance are slight. As might be expected, the company to which you apply will ask whether you have ever received benefits under any accident and health insurance, and whether any insurance has ever been declined, canceled, or refused renewal by any other company. Your history with the previous company will weigh heavily against you.

Even if you manage to obtain a new policy, the rates will almost always be considerably higher than under the policy you had been carrying. Frequently, if your application for the new policy sets forth a medical condition or impairment which you have developed, the new policy will not be issued unless you consent to its bearing a rider excluding benefits for the "pre-existing condition." Even if no waiver of this kind is asked, most policies are not liable for recurrence of conditions which originated before the policies were written. In this situation it is worthwhile to check on the availability of "substandard" coverage, which is designed to accommodate a pre-existing condition at a higher premium.

Group policies usually superior

A limitation on benefits can prove extremely important in any disability insurance plan. It is on this score, as well as on the factor of costs, that many group accident and health policies are superior to individually purchased contracts. If you enroll in a group policy immediately after beginning new employment, no health examination is required.

Disability by Income Group

Family Income in 1974	Types of Disability		
	Restricted Activity	Bed Disability	Work-Loss Days
	Days per person per year		
All Incomes	17.2	6.7	4.9
Under $ 3,000	35.9	13.2	6.9
$ 3,000-$ 4,999	25.9	9.8	7.0
$ 5,000-$ 6,999	21.2	8.4	6.6
$ 7,000-$ 9,999	16.4	6.4	5.7
$10,000-$14,999	13.9	5.5	4.8
$15,000-$24,999	12.4	4.9	4.2
$25,000 And Over	10.8	3.9	3.3

Sources: Health Insurance Institute, U.S. Department of Health, Education, and Welfare

Once a claim has arisen under your policy, this claim must be settled in full, regardless of whether the policy is cancelable or calls for renewal only with the company's consent at the end of each year. To this extent, you can count on collecting in full on the first claim you present under a cancelable policy. If your contract is of the more liberal variety which can be terminated by the company only at the end of the year, you are assured of collecting on all claims that may arise within any one policy year.

The serious defect in either type of policy lies in the fact that you cannot depend on having any further insurance after these initial periods. Since most chronic illnesses are preceded by periods of temporary disability, there is always the risk that you will lose the policy before the long-term disability sets in. Even a first attack of any disease or condition that threatens to be chronic may convince the company that you are an impaired risk. Furthermore, even if there is no threat of a chronic infirmity, a series of recurrent illnesses of short duration may also mark you as a poor risk. In fact, the company could cancel or refuse renewal of a policy before you ever presented a claim if it learned of some condition which threatened your continued good health.

Causes of cancellation

The right of the company to cancel or refuse renewal is often defended on the grounds that it provides a safeguard against the "moral hazard" in this branch of insurance. Underwriting this risk, some contend, cannot be handled effectively unless there is a way to eliminate those who obtain policies by fraud or misstatement and those who are dishonest in making claims.

There is no question that these factors enter into any consideration of cancelable insurance, but they do not tell the whole story. While there are no definitive statistics on the number of policies that are terminated for different reasons, accident and health policies actually are canceled or refused renewal because the insured has become an impaired risk. An authoritative study[1] on health insurance cites five "principal causes of cancellation." Two of the reasons given are "impaired physical condition" and "repeated claims for recurrent types of diseases."

There are countless illnesses or medical conditions which might bring you within these groups. You would then face possible loss of your policy regardless of how many years you had been making regular payments on it.

The cancelable or nonrenewable policy evidently is drawn up so that the company would have the option to "get off the risk." This is not to say that accident and health companies will pay only one claim or that they withdraw from a policy

1. Laird, John M., "Non-Cancelable Accident and Health Insurance Underwriting Problems," *Proceedings* of the Casualty Actuarial Society, Vol. VII, pt. 2, p. 306.

as soon as they have reason to expect a claim. Most companies try to conduct their business in a manner that serves their insured clientele as widely as is consistent with profitable underwriting, and they have paid out a large part of their receipts in the form of benefits.

But to you, as an individual who may suffer a disabling injury or illness at any time, one question remains paramount: "Is there any accident and sickness insurance that can be counted on to provide a regular income when it is needed?"

For this, you require a policy which you can retain at your sole option, at least through the productive period of life. You will recall that a similar question arose in connection with renewable life insurance. We observed that a policy to cover the productive period should carry you at least until age sixty-five with the option of renewal in your hands throughout that time. Is there any accident and health insurance that fulfills this requirement?

Renewable policies

There is some *guaranteed renewable* health and accident insurance which may be carried until a relatively advanced age. While some renewable accident and health policies grant the insured the option to renew only until he attains age fifty or fifty-five, there are many companies issuing policies renewable to age sixty and sixty-five.

As a general rule, most renewable policies are sold only to "preferred" occupations. Heavy or hazardous trades are ineligible, and general practice restricts this insurance to business, professional, and white-collar groups. Some policies are issued to workers employed in skilled and supervisory capacities in certain industries. In recent years insurance companies have increasingly offered noncancelable and guaranteed renewable insurance to women. In all cases, there is rigid scrutiny of the health, habits, and financial situation of the prospect.

Two distinct categories

Although the distinction would appear at first to be purely semantic, the insurance industry has developed two categories for renewable policies. A policy which is only guaranteed renewable may be renewed by the policyholder at his sole option until he attains the maximum age stated in the contract. Such policies may, however, be subject to an increase in rate. It is usually provided that the rate will be changed only if the entire class to which the insured belongs is subjected to a revision, and this must usually be justified by the company to the regulatory authorities of the state on the basis of its actual experience with that class of business.

A policy may also be noncancelable, in which case the insured is assured not only of its renewability but also of the continuance of the insurance at the same rate as when the policy was issued.

In addition to these two varieties of renewable contracts, there are policies (mostly of an older vintage) which impose a maximum limit on all claims which will be paid in the aggregate over the entire life of the policy. While these contracts are noncancelable in the strict sense, a policyholder can find himself without any further protection after he has exhausted the dollar maximum imposed by the policy provisions.

While the field is somewhat circumscribed, there are many desirable policies which will pay income for life on disabling injuries and to age sixty-five when the policyholder is disabled by illness. Such policies must, however, be reviewed carefully because they differ widely on many important phases of their coverage.

For one thing, there are variations in the amount of indemnity payable under different circumstances. A number of special benefits also vary from policy to policy. Some policies stipulate that you be unable to perform the duties of your regular occupation; others pay benefits only if you are prevented from following any occupation; and in some policies these requirements are combined.

The confining clause

A few policies still pay reduced or limited benefits for disabilities which do not confine the insured totally and continuously within doors. A clause of this kind may be of considerable importance, particularly in contracts which are purchased to cover long-term disabilities, for relatively few conditions which render a person disabled over a long period of time are likely to confine him continuously within doors.

During the past decade, in the face of the refusal of the courts to apply the confining clause strictly according to its phraseology, this type of clause has begun to fall into disuse. Since this clause was more widely used in older policies, it would be wise for you to check any policies you may be carrying as well as any new contracts that are offered to you to determine whether this trap for the unwary is in the policy provisions. The clause states quite simply that the full benefit will be paid only while the insured is continuously confined within doors. If not confined, the benefit may be reduced or its duration curtailed or eliminated entirely. A clause of this type is a serious defect in a plan to cover long-term disabilities. In general, policies with a clause of this type should be avoided.

But more important than these distinctions are the serious differences in the length of time you can collect under the various contracts. In accident and health insurance, the amount of protection you receive is naturally affected by the period of time for which the policy will indemnify you. Three contracts may each be written to pay $500 a month, but in the first this benefit may be payable for life, in the second for no more than twelve months on any single claim, and in the third for a total of twelve months on all claims.

Another important difference in policies is the elimination of the initial periods of disability. Thus, one policy may pay from the first day of an accident and from the eighth day of a disability arising from an illness. This is known in the insurance business as 0-7. Policies may carry elimination periods of seven days for either accident or illness, or eliminate the first two weeks, or the first thirty days, or some other period. In noncancelable insurance, it is not unusual to find as much as 180 days eliminated for accidents and illnesses, although the common period is thirty days.

Notify the company without delay

Even though your policy may not provide benefits for the first thirty days or longer of any disability, you must not delay until the waiting period is over to notify the company of your disabling injury or illness.

You should send written notice of your illness or injury to

the company as soon after the disability commences as is possible. All policies contain a provision which requires that written notice of injury or sickness on which a claim may be based must be given to the company within twenty days after the date of the accident causing the injury or of the commencement of disability from sickness.

Some states have extended the time during which the insured is allowed to notify the company of disabling injury or illness, but the safest course to follow is to notify the company immediately of any accidental injury or illness that you suffer even though your policy contains a long waiting period and may not be called on at all to pay benefits for the particular disability.

If you have notified the company of a disability or have filed a claim for benefits or have begun to collect monthly benefits under your policy, do not assume that you can stop paying premiums. Some accident and health policies provide that premiums be waived during disability or when benefits are being paid; others make no such stipulation. Some allow premiums to be waived only after disability has continued for a stated number of months, even though benefits have begun to be paid.

Thus, a policy may begin to pay benefits on the ninety-first day of a disability, but premiums may not be waived until the disability has been continuous for as much as six consecutive months. Under such a policy, any premium that falls due before the disability has continued for six months must be paid to avoid lapse.

If you are receiving benefits under a claim on your policy, continue to pay all premiums as they fall due until you satisfy yourself concerning the waiver-of-premium provisions incorporated in your policy. Otherwise, you may find that your policy has lapsed for nonpayment of premiums. This will not affect the claim that has already risen under your policy, but your insurance against all future claims may be lost irretrievably.

The policy provides the company with the right to examine you when and as often as it may reasonably require during the period of the claim, and you must notify the company every six months that you are still disabled.

Work Days Lost Due to Acute Conditions

	Work Days Lost Per Employed Person in 1974		
	All Ages 17 and Over	Age 17-44	Age 45 and Over
Both Sexes			
All acute conditions	3.4	3.5	3.2
Infective and parasitic diseases	0.2	0.3	0.2
Respiratory conditions	1.5	1.5	1.4
Digestive system conditions	0.2	0.2	0.2
Injuries	1.0	1.0	1.0
All other acute conditions	0.5	0.5	0.5
Male			
All acute conditions	3.2	3.2	3.2
Infective and parasitic diseases	0.2	0.2	*
Respiratory conditions	1.3	1.4	1.2
Digestive system conditions	0.2	0.2	*
Injuries	1.2	1.2	1.3
All other acute conditions	0.4	0.3	0.4
Female			
All acute conditions	3.6	3.8	3.2
Infective and parasitic diseases	0.3	0.3	*
Respiratory conditions	1.7	1.8	1.6
Digestive system conditions	0.2	0.2	*
Injuries	0.7	0.7	0.5
All other acute conditions	0.7	0.7	0.7

*Figures do not meet standards of reliability or precision.

Sources: Health Insurance Institute, U.S. Department of Health, Education, and Welfare

Carrying additional policies

If you carry more than one policy providing benefits for accidental injury or illness, it is extremely important that you give written notice to the companies of the existence of other insurance. This applies to any policy or certificate or other provision for this form of coverage. If you fail to comply with this recommendation, you may find yourself collecting only a fraction of the benefits stipulated in your policy because policies usually carry a provision which limits liability when you have already collected for the same disability.

Commonly, a policy limits the amount of total indemnity which may be carried in all policies in relation to the average earnings of the insured. Under a clause of this kind, if your average earnings for the two years prior to your claim did not exceed the total benefits payable from all your policies or certificates of accident, health, or disability insurance, the company's liability is limited to a proportionate share of the indemnity. This share is determined by the ratio that your average earnings during the two year period bear to the promised benefits in all your policies.

When you apply for a policy, notify the company of all existing accident and health contracts and certificates and other disability protection in any life insurance. Also inform all other companies which have issued policies to you of the new addition to your disability protection. This is necessary because a clause in a policy requiring you to notify the company of other insurance applies not only to policies you are already carrying but also to any insurance you may purchase at a later date. However, this requirement does not apply to guaranteed renewable insurance.

Do not rely on reminders

It is important that you understand that your accident and health insurance company may not be required to mail regular notices of the premium due under your policy. Otherwise, you may rely entirely on a reminder from the company which may not come. If you fail to pay your premium by the end of the grace period, your policy will lapse. Its reinstatement once it has lapsed is optional with the company, which could refuse to accept any further premiums. If your policy should lapse, the insurance company must nevertheless pay any lawful claim incurred while the policy was in force.

If you pay your premiums on a weekly basis, you can expect to have a grace period of up to six days. Payments made on a monthly basis are allowed a grace period of up to ten days, and payments made quarterly, semiannually, or annually have a maximum grace period of thirty-one days.

You should make a note of the premium date of your accident and health policy and pay the premium in time. Since so much depends on renewability, it is important that you guard against any possibility of losing your policy through failure to pay a premium when it falls due.

To keep premium costs in line, your policy can be written with a longer elimination period, such as 90 days or even 180 days. A policy of this kind may not apply to the greatest number of disabilities but it does shift to the risk-bearing institution the more severe economic losses which few of us can absorb without hardship.

Any consideration of protecting against the hazard of short-term disability must wait on your having estimated the long-term coverage under Social Security and any group policies available to you and on your having made provision for the heavier medical expenses that can prove economically crippling. You may find that your financial resources and coverage sponsored at your place of employment (as well as the temporary disability insurance mandated by your state) greatly reduce or even obviate the need to procure individual insurance against short-term disability.

CHAPTER 10

Covering
Major
Medical
Expenses

Medical costs have shown the largest percentage increase of all the major groups of expenditures in the Consumer Price Index during the past two decades. Today, relatively few families possess enough personal funds to meet the expenses involved in a severe accident or illness without hardship.

Many illnesses and accidents entail some stay in a hospital. In an effort to spread the risk of heavy expenses that usually attend hospital confinement, insurance companies, independent plans, and hospital service plans such as Blue Cross have proliferated. It is estimated that over 80 percent of the American people are covered by some form of hospital protection. There is wide diversity in coverage among these policies but they all revolve around the expenses that are incurred for a hospital stay.

A relative newcomer to this field of insurance is the major

medical expense policy. This type of contract does not focus on hospital-connected expenses but rather covers all medical and surgical costs. Generally, no distinction is made between hospital charges and those incurred outside these institutions. The policy fills the requirement stressed in the preceding chapters on accident and sickness insurance: the first risk to be covered is the "catastrophe"—the one that cannot be met out of resources, that cannot be budgeted for successfully.

No policy pays all expenses

While no major medical policy undertakes to pay all the medical expenses incurred by the policyholder, and despite many important differences among contracts offered by the various companies, they are all designed to shift to the insurer the larger portion of the expenses that result from accidents or illnesses.

Every major medical policy incorporates a deductible, an initial amount which the insured person has to pay before the policy comes into play. Deductibles range from less than $100 to more than $1,000. Some companies offer the insured person a choice of deductibles, while others restrict his options in relation to his earnings. In any event, there is no reimbursement until the expenses exceed the deductible. Many policies have now added a modifying provision which places a maximum on the amount of the deductible when several members of the same family are involved in an accident or suffer from a contagious disease.

Major medical policies usually exclude coverage for medical expenses incurred because of accidents or occupational illnesses which are covered under the Workmen's Compensation statutes of any state. They usually also omit coverage for loss arising out of war, and may limit reimbursement for mental and nervous disorders. A few contracts also exclude some other situations, but basically the policies are designed to apply to almost all the usual medical, surgical, hospital, and related expenses.

All major medical policies have the insured person share in the payment on a percentage basis. A fairly common clause of this kind provides that the company will bear 80 percent of the charges above the deductible. Some companies pay only

Personal Spending for Medical Care
(Percent in 1974)

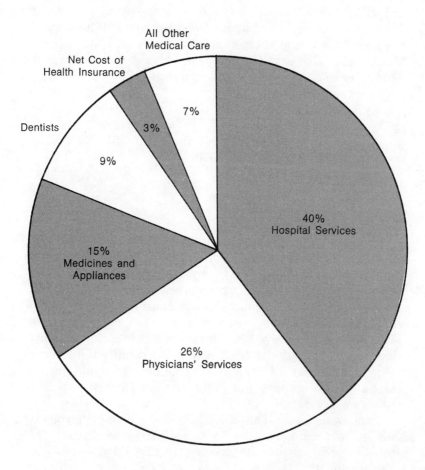

All Other
Medical Care

Net Cost of
Health Insurance

Dentists

7%

3%

9%

40%
Hospital Services

15%
Medicines and
Appliances

26%
Physicians' Services

Sources: U.S. Department of Commerce, Health Insurance Institute

75 percent of such covered charges, while others offer a clause under which the policyholder's participation decreases as total expenses increase. Thus, the policy may provide for a $500 deductible, with the company agreeing to pay 80 percent of the first $1,000 incurred above the deductible, 90 percent of the next $2,000, and 100 percent thereafter. A policy of this kind would reimburse the policyholder in a situation where he incurred $7,500 of medical expenses as follows:

Amount Paid
By Insured
$500 Deductible
  200 20% of first $1,000 above deductible
  200 10% of next $2,000
$ 900 Paid by insured
$6,600 Paid by company

Time to reach the deductible

Commonly, policies state that they will pay all expenses above the deductible sum if this figure is reached within 120 days. Some policies allow sixty days, ninety days, six months, or a full year as the time in which to reach the deductible. The coverage under these clauses varies considerably. Thus, assume your medical expense policy agrees to indemnify for all medical expenses above $500 incurred within a sixty-day period. If you were under treatment for a condition and your medical bills totaled $200 a month, the insurer would not become involved because you did not incur $500 of expenses within a sixty-day period.

In the same medical situation, a policy which gave you six months to accumulate the $500 deductible would pay the stated percentage of all expenses incurred by you beginning during the third month of your course of treatment when you had spent $500. All expenses above this amount as they were met each month would be covered under the policy.

All major medical policies have a stated dollar maximum, usually ranging from $10,000 to $100,000. Most companies offer larger maximums in policies which include a large deductible. These policies are designed for persons in the high-income group.

It is important to be aware that the maximum amount

The Rising Cost of Medical Care
(1967 = 100 in the Consumer Price Index)

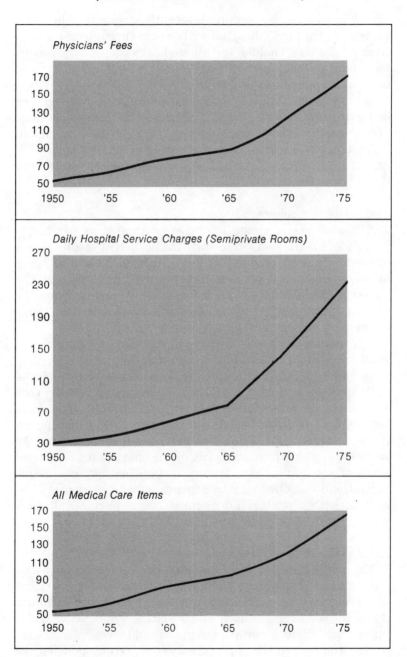

Source: U.S. Department of Labor

stated in policies may apply differently. In some policies, it represents the maximum that will be paid throughout the lifetime of the policyholder for all medical expenses. However, most policies promise to pay the stipulated maximum for any one continuous illness or condition.

Some policies require that the insured person absorb the deductible amount in a single illness or accident situation; others require that he merely reach the deductible amount in a given period of time, regardless of how many separate illnesses are involved. Clearly a policy of the latter type is more liberal than the former.

Limitations on coverage

Although major medical policies originated as devices to permit an insured person to shift the burden of medical costs above a stipulated deductible to an insurance carrier, many of these contracts have now incorporated limitations on the coverage they offer. This is accomplished by enumerating the "covered charges." All charges which fall outside the scope of these definitions are not covered.

The most important of these limitations, and the one found most frequently, relates to coverage for the cost of a private room in a hospital. The majority of major medical policies— with some outstanding exceptions—specifically provide that the policy will not consider as a covered expense any charge for hospital room and board which exceeds the normal charge made by that hospital for semiprivate accommodations. In some cities, the difference between the charges for these two types of room and board is very large. How important this limitation in a policy may be depends on whether you will be content with a semiprivate room if you require hospitalization.

Savings in group policy

The majority of policies covering major medical expense (and similar policies of a comprehensive nature) are written on a group basis. In addition to important savings in premium due to the economies of mass underwriting, employers usually make a contribution toward the premium, thereby further reducing the cost to the covered employee. Group policies are also generally more liberal in their coverage of medical expenses incurred in connection with preexisting conditions.

In all instances, where group insurance is available to you, the coverage should be checked before you buy an individual policy. Group coverage in this field is beset by some of the drawbacks that were pointed out in the chapter dealing with group life insurance, the most important being that the employee may find himself without coverage and uninsurable when his employment terminates.

New York State has enacted a statute which gives the employee the right to convert to a hospitalization policy without evidence of insurability. As a result of legislation passed in 1975, the guarantee covers representative benefits, even though they are somewhat below those in the group insurance carried during the period of employment.

A case might be made for trying to obtain and maintain individual major medical policies for yourself and members of your family even when a group policy is available to you, but in view of the fact that group policies are generally broader and less expensive than those in the individual field, the employer-sponsored program is usually the better option. This may involve a calculated risk, it is true, but it is probably advisable unless your employment is insecure or the group policy is too circumscribed in its provisions.

Assessing individual policies

There is considerable variation among the major medical policies offered by the carriers—life insurance companies, accident and health plans, and casualty insurers. In assessing the products being offered if you are buying an individual policy, you should take into account the amount of the deductible; the period of time during which the deductible must be reached in order for the policy to become involved; whether it is a per cause or a per time deductible; and whether the maximum payable under the policy is based on each claim or is a lifetime maximum.

The policy you buy will have to fit into your budget and, as a consequence, you may have to compromise in some of the areas it covers. You should strive first to obtain a policy with a high maximum. A $10,000 maximum *per cause* might be considered a minimum; if the maximum is applied over all causes throughout the lifetime of the policyholder, a maximum of about $100,000 should be considered.

Every effort should be made to procure a policy with a deductible which can be satisfied within a calendar year or in a period not less than six months.

Finally, the "inside limits" that the policy may include should be checked carefully. If the policy contains dollar limits on all types of situations, it is hardly able to accomplish the purpose for which major medical was first conceived—to put a top limit on the amount of medical expenses the policyholder and his family will have to pay out of their own resources.

Hospitalization contracts

After you have covered your family group with the most comprehensive major medical policy at your place of work or on an individual basis, you will be able to estimate the medical expenses you might have to pay. If you find that this self-insured sector of medical bills is still too high for your financial comfort, you can consider closing the gap by acquiring a hospitalization contract.

Many groups are covered under both types of policies—a hospital plan with a major medical policy superimposed on it. A group major medical policy generally carries a "corridor" deductible which eliminates $50 or $100 of expenses above the amounts paid under the hospital policy. A health insurance program of this kind should suffice to bring all but the most unusual medical expense situations into manageable proportions.

Where group coverage is unavailable and you find that you need to supplement the major medical policy you have purchased on an individual basis, you can take out a hospital expense policy.

Here again, the contracts should be studied carefully to make sure that they are free of severely limiting exclusions and that they provide adequate coverage for "miscellaneous" services, which can develop fairly substantial costs, e.g., anesthesia, use of the operating room, X-rays, blood transfusions, and drugs.

Most hospital policies offer some coverage for the cost of surgery the patient may undergo, usually with a set of fees stipulated for each type of operation. Competitive policies should be compared on this score, for many are written with totally inadequate schedules in light of the surgery fees being charged.

If a hospital policy and a major medical policy are both to be maintained, it is important that the major medical policy be written with a deductible which is high enough to avoid duplicating the benefits available under the basic hospital contract. Otherwise, there is an unwarranted premium expenditure.

Hospital service plans

The hospital service plan is actually a contract among three parties—the insured, the plan, and a group of hospitals.

The plan agrees to provide the participant with a stated number of days of accommodations within any one year—twenty-one days, thirty days, sixty days, ninety days, and so forth. Some plans will allow full benefits for a stated number of days followed by half benefits for additional days.

A few plans grant these services for any one disability or single admission regardless of previous benefits received during the year. In addition, these plans allow for some miscellaneous hospital services, such as use of the operating room, anesthesia, X-rays, dressings, and special treatments.

As indicated, the number of days for which full coverage is provided differs widely among the plans. Many plans allow for continued service after these periods at reduced rates. The percentage of discount for additional days varies among the plans, as does the number of additional days provided.

In certain plans, hospitalization is provided for almost any condition; others eliminate mental ailments, tuberculosis, and quarantinable diseases. All plans exclude service for conditions which are covered by Workmen's Compensation or federal liability laws. Preexisting conditions are barred under some plans, while others permit service for such conditions after stipulated periods. There are also differences in the hospital accommodations made available and variations in the benefits offered to dependents.

More Receiving Hospital Care

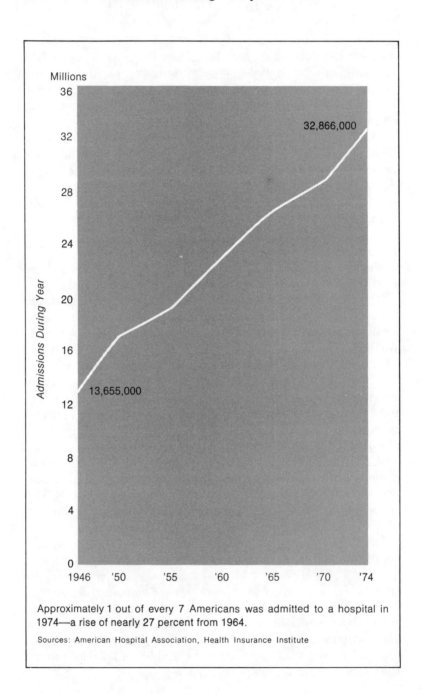

Millions

32,866,000

13,655,000

Admissions During Year

1946   '50   '55   '60   '65   '70   '74

Approximately 1 out of every 7 Americans was admitted to a hospital in 1974—a rise of nearly 27 percent from 1964.

Sources: American Hospital Association, Health Insurance Institute

Insofar as any generalization is possible from the mass of cash indemnity and service plans, it is fairly safe to conclude that the nonprofit hospital associations offering services charge lower rates than the commercial companies which provide cash indemnities.

In many instances, a subscriber to a service plan will find his coverage more convenient than the cash indemnity plan. Under the latter, the patient may be required to put down a deposit before being admitted to a hospital and to pay his bill before discharge, and then file a claim with the insurer for reimbursement. However, many companies have now filed data with the hospitals on their policies, particularly the group plans, and an insured person is often admitted without any cash advance. Under the service plan, there is usually no question about the applicability of the coverage, especially if the patient is being admitted to a member or participating hospital. His membership card is usually enough to gain him admission to the hospital, and his bill is paid directly to the hospital by the plan.

Blue Cross groups

There are some service plans operated by private hospitals, but the bulk of these plans are community organized and operate on a statewide or county basis. These plans are usually known as Blue Cross and are approved by the American Hospital Association. Blue Cross hospital service plans now serve every state except Hawaii.

Many Blue Cross plans accept only group enrollment, although a few urban plans provide for individual subscribers where no group membership is possible. It is important to remember, however, that Blue Cross groups need not always be employee groups such as those required for regular group insurance. Residents of small towns can often join through community enrollment, and farmers can subscribe through farm bureaus, granges, unions, and county health associations. Consumer cooperatives and unions often act as enrollment centers. Furthermore, Blue Cross plans will often allow one person to act as a central collection agency for all members in his place of employment.

If you are self-employed or do not work with a sizable

group, there are Blue Cross plans which will accept your membership on a direct basis. Some plans enroll self-employed individuals during certain months of the year.

Blue Shield plans offer a service in which participating doctors accept the Blue Shield allowance as full payment for their services if the insured person's income is below a specified limit. The services covered are usually surgery and hospital treatment although some illnesses which do not require hospitalization are being covered by an increasing number of these plans.

Health maintenance organizations

Over the years, numerous organizations have offered medical services on a group-practice basis in a way that is calculated to make the dispensing of these services more economical. The movement has received added impetus in the last few years, and numerous "health maintenance organizations" now offer virtually complete medical services to their members or subscribers.

Almost all of these programs are geared toward groups which have an affiliation either on a trade or a regional basis. Several of these programs have been in operation for many years and are firmly established. Among these are the Kaiser Foundation Health Plan, originally set up on an industry basis but now operating communitywide, owning twelve hospitals and over forty outpatient medical centers. The Health Insurance Plan of Greater New York and Group Health Insurance of New York are two other well-established plans operating on a community basis. Several trade unions operate similar service-type organizations.

On the West Coast and in the Middle West, a number of medical corporations have been set up by county medical societies and these have developed fee schedules which are accepted as full payment by physicians participating in the plan. There are also private group clinics, many of which are comparatively small, although some, such as the Ross-Loos Medical Group of Los Angeles, have achieved considerable stature. Another large and highly regarded consumer-sponsored association of this kind is the Group Health Association of Washington, D.C.

If you are eligible for participation in one of these "independent" plans, you might give it serious consideration. Affiliating yourself with a plan of this kind could protect you against the more severe medical expenses that may be incurred by your family.

Medicare benefits

In 1965, a program of medical care for the aged was added to Social Security. Benefits are provided for all persons who are sixty-five or over and also to certain Social Security disability beneficiaries under sixty-five. This extension of Social Security is popularly known as Medicare. It consists of two sets of benefits. A basic hospitalization coverage is provided, financed out of the contributions made by workers and employers to Social Security. Supplementary Medical Insurance Benefits for the Aged, a voluntary plan available to all persons over sixty-five, adds to the benefits under the basic plan. To this supplementary program, the covered participant contributes a monthly premium charge (which is deducted from his monthly benefits under Social Security).

Most medical care insurance is now being drawn to reduce benefits when the insured person becomes eligible for Medicare. Because of this and of the fact that the Supplementary Medical Insurance Benefits are furnished at a very attractive premium, persons who attain age sixty-five, even if their individual or group medical care insurance continues beyond that point, are generally advised to enroll for the supplementary protection. Enrollment should be undertaken as soon as possible to avoid postponement of the date on which benefits become effective. The law stipulates that persons who do not enroll within certain periods after attaining eligibility will be subject to waiting periods.

Buying policies by mail

There are a large number of hospitalization and accident and health policies sold by mail. Before you buy such a policy, it is advisable to make sure that the company is licensed in your home state. This is necessary because there is nothing to prevent a company from soliciting and selling insurance by mail in states in which it is not licensed. Many companies in this field are actually licensed in only one state and in some instances obsolete charters exclude them from any supervision in their home state.

There is nothing wrong with selling and buying insurance by mail, and many responsible companies have been transacting such business for years. What is important to bear in mind is that buying insurance from a company which is not licensed in your state may deny you the protection of your state insurance department's supervision of the company's reserves, policies, and underwriting practices. In the event of a dispute between you and the company, your state insurance department may be powerless or severely hampered in its ability to help you.

This point is far from academic. For years, a group of unscrupulous companies preyed on unsuspecting mail-order purchasers. The situation improved considerably after the Federal Trade Commission stepped into the supervision of the advertising claims made by insurance carriers.

Formerly, if it became necessary to bring a suit against an out-of-state company which was not licensed in your state, it would entail traveling to the state where the company was domiciled. Now, about two-thirds of the states have enacted laws which make it possible for you to serve a summons on the superintendent of insurance of your own state on behalf of the company in question. The extent of the security this type of law affords is still somewhat uncertain, and it would therefore be best for you to make your choice from among the licensed carriers in your state.

To ascertain whether a company is licensed in your state, write to your state insurance department. This bureau is located in your state's capital in all cases except in California and Illinois, where Los Angeles and Chicago are the respective seats of the department.

PART THREE
Your Retirement Program

11

When
You Need
an Annuity

The economic risk of "living too long," as it has been called, faces all people, and sooner or later we must come to grips with the problem of security in old age.

The most direct way to meet the financial needs of your old age would be to set aside during the earlier, productive period of your life sufficient reserves to take care of your later years. However, the amount of money needed to provide a measure of comfort after retirement is large, and only a relatively small number of persons can hope to accumulate such reserves.

Most people, after passing the productive period of life, have to depend at least for part of their support on other sources—Social Security retirement benefits, industrial pension plans or retirement systems at their place of employment, income from a business, commissions, royalties, and any other revenue they can expect to receive after retirement.

For many people, however, the combined income from such sources may be inadequate to provide an acceptable minimum necessary for their maintenance. In such cases they could not afford to retire, and they would be forced to continue working. If advanced age precluded continued employment, they might have to depend on the bounty of others or appeal for public charity.

Annuity contracts

The gap between the minimum income you require and the revenue you can expect after retirement may be filled by the purchase of a special contract from a life insurance company. Such contracts, usually called annuities, are designed to provide a guaranteed income which cannot be outlived.

When you consider retiring from active work, you will take into account the yield you can expect from your assets and investments, including revenue you can draw from any business or property which you own, pensions to which you are entitled, and retirement benefits for which you may be eligible under Social Security.

If you find that the returns on your accumulated funds are sufficient to provide an adequate income for your retirement, you may have no need for the annuity plans offered by life insurance companies. You could feel secure in your declining years, however, only if these savings were large enough to provide a regular income throughout your lifetime when invested conservatively. Any element of speculation in the investment of such life savings would be a source of danger to the income on which you must depend for support.

It is fairly easy to see that large sums of money would have to be invested in order to provide even a modest income. If we take 6 percent as a safe yield on your capital, an income of $5,000 a year, a little under $100 a week, will require an investment of over $83,000. Not many people find themselves in a position to secure even this extremely frugal standard of living from accumulated savings.

Old-age benefits under Social Security

The amount of money you have accumulated may not in itself be sufficient to provide an adequate retirement income but it may supplement other retirement benefits to which you are entitled. In the retirement program of most wage earners, it is the old-age benefits under Social Security which play the most important part. The precise Social Security benefits to which a worker is entitled differ with the individual case, but a brief outline of some of the provisions will give you an idea of the retirement benefits for which you may be eligible.

Most wage earners are working in occupations covered by Social Security. There are certain groups which are outside the scope of the act. For the most part, these include sectors of the population covered under other retirement programs, e.g., federal employees. The noncovered groups account for some 10 percent of the working population. Other gainfully employed individuals will find that their pay envelope or salary check shows a deduction for Social Security.

Broadly, you are required to work in a covered occupation at least 25 percent of the time between 1950 and the year before you attain age sixty-two. If your twenty-first birthday occurred in a year after 1950, then the requirement is based on the number of years that will have elapsed after that year and the year before you reach sixty-two. Put more precisely, a worker, to be eligible, needs at least one quarter of coverage for each calendar year in the period described. A quarter of coverage, you will recall, is one in which a worker is paid at least $50 in wages or receives $400 (counting for four quarters) from self-employment.

When a worker has forty quarters of coverage, he is permanently insured and eligible for retirement benefits. These benefits vary for the individual worker and his dependents. They are based on his average earnings during the years he was employed and deductions were being made towards Social Security.

To cite one example as a frame of reference. If you will reach age sixty-five in 1978 or later and you have been employed all through your qualifying years in covered occupations paying at least the maximum amount subject to deductions (ranging from $15,300 on earnings starting in 1976 down to $3,600 for the years 1951 through 1954), you will be entitled to a monthly income of $432.40; if your wife is the

Social Security Coverage

(000 omitted)

Year	Employer and Worker Taxes	Persons Fully Insured	Persons Receiving Monthly Benefits	Monthly and Lump-Sum Payments
1940	$ 637,000	24,200	222	$ 35,354
1945	1,285,486	33,400	1,288	273,885
1950	2,667,077	59,800	3,478	961,094
1955	5,713,045	70,500	7,960	4,968,155
1960	11,876,220	84,400	14,844	11,244,795
1965	17,205,372	94,800	20,867	18,310,676
1966	22,585,229	97,200	22,767	20,048,347
1967	25,423,792	99,900	23,707	21,406,455
1968	27,034,289	102,600	24,562	24,936,435
1969	31,545,608	105,400	25,314	26,750,841
1970	34,737,059	108,200	26,229	31,863,381
1971	38,342,721	110,600	27,291	37,170,726
1972	42,888,228	113,200	28,476	41,595,064
1973	51,907,100	115,900	29,868	51,459,310
1974	58,906,800	118,100	30,854	58,521,345
1975	64,259,000	123,000	32,085	66,922,707

Sources: Social Security Administration, Institute of Life Insurance

same age, your combined monthly income will total $648.60.

Restriction on earnings

You will recall that there is a restriction on the amount of money that may be earned by a beneficiary without suffering a decrease in benefits. Basically, there is no reduction if a recipient earns no more than $2,760 in a year; for each $2 earned during a year above this figure, $1 in benefits is deducted, except that the full benefit is paid for any month in which not more than $230 is earned. All restrictions on earning income are removed for beneficiaries who are seventy-two or older. You should bear in mind that the limitations apply to earnings from wages or self-employment but not to income from investments.

The law provides for automatic annual increase in benefits, proportionate to any increase in average annual taxable wages in the country.

If you want assistance with estimating your retirement benefits, you may call at your local office of the Social Security Administration. An easy-to-follow brochure is available to help you calculate your benefits (DHEW Publication No. (SSA) 73-10047).

The Social Security limitation on earned income can be of considerable importance in your retirement program. If you conclude, as many individuals do, that you will need to supplement your Social Security checks by gainful employment, you may find yourself forgoing some portion of your government-sponsored retirement benefits. Supplementing your Social Security benefits without outside employment is a worthwhile goal in planning for your retirement because the loss of even a portion of your benefits can prove very costly.

Other pension plans for employees

The period since World War II has witnessed a great expansion of industry-sponsored pension plans. About half of the employed population can now look forward not only to monthly income from Social Security but also to a lifetime income from a pension plan at their place of employment. The combination of these two pension schemes may meet the minimum needs of a retired worker and his dependents.

Of course, an industry-controlled pension may depend on your continued employment in a particular job until your retirement. But even if you leave the job, if you have been employed for some time you may be entitled to some "vesting" in the contributions which have been made on your behalf.

After arriving at a figure for all old-age benefits to which you will be entitled under Social Security and private pension plans, there may still be a gap in your retirement needs. This gap may be filled from the savings you have been able to accumulate during the productive years of your working life. But if you are to be sure of a continuous income which cannot be outlived, you will have to use only the interest or investment yield of such funds. If you are forced to withdraw part of the capital you have saved in order to meet your living expenses, you will face the risk of exhausting these funds. You will not have the security which is basic to a retirement program, for such security calls for a guaranteed income that cannot be outlived.

What often happens when savings are insufficient to support an aged person or to supplement other retirement benefits is that he is compelled to make steady inroads into the capital he has set aside. As the principal grows smaller, the interest declines, and the withdrawals from the fund must grow larger. The retirement funds threaten to vanish as the years go by. The economic risk of "living too long" then becomes a real hazard.

Outliving your savings

The risk of outliving the savings which can be accumulated in an average lifetime faces almost everyone to one degree or another. Not all people contemplating the uncertainties of retirement will live to the same age. Many will be removed by death within relatively short periods of time, while others will live to ages far above the average.

It is at this point that the insurance principle can be put to work. For if all people who are at the point of retirement were to pool their resources, a guaranteed income could be assured to all for as long as they live. Those who die early would pay for the ones who live on. Everyone in the group would be free of the haunting fear of "living too long."

Naturally, the amount of income paid to each member per $1,000 of investment would depend on the returns that the money could earn and on the mortality experienced by such groups.

The pooling of the resources of a large number of retirees to guarantee an income to each member of the group throughout his lifetime involves the principle of life expectancy and it therefore falls to the life insurance company to make this device workable.

Let us see how a plan of this kind may fit into your financial charting. Assuming that your Social Security benefits at retirement will amount to $550 per month, you find that you will need at least $150 a month additional income to maintain yourself in minimum comfort.

To purchase this supplementary retirement income from a typical insurance company at age sixty-five will cost some $17,000 for a male and about $21,000 for a female. These same sums, invested at 5 percent interest, would yield about $80 a month (based on the $17,000) or about $87 (on the $21,000), which you would find inadequate for supplementing your other retirement income.

This type of contract which agrees to furnish you with a definite monthly income for life in exchange for a lump-sum payment is commonly called an annuity. Strictly, the amount of income to be received by you each year is the annuity, but common usage extends the word to the contract purchased from an insurance company.

Stretching retirement funds

The annuity contract, as we have seen, can be used to supplement a retirement income from other sources. It can also be used to provide the full retirement income you require or a more limited pension which can free you in part from the burden of earning a living at the older ages. For all people, the annuity offers a method of stretching retirement funds to provide an income that is free from the threat of exhaustion.

The amount of income you will obtain under an annuity contract will depend on your age at the time of purchase. Rates are quoted for each age and separately for men and women. Women receive a smaller annual income than men

Number of Persons Covered by Major Pension And Retirement Programs in United States

(000 omitted)

| Year | Social Security | Private Plans | |
		With Life Insurance Companies	Other Private Plans
1930	—	100	2,700
1935	—	285	2,525
1940	27,622	695	3,565
1945	40,488	1,470	5,240
1950	44,477	2,755	7,500
1955	64,161	4,105	12,290
1960	73,845	5,475	17,540
1965	87,267	7,040	21,060
1966	91,768	7,835	21,640
1967	93,607	8,700	22,280
1968	95,862	9,155	22,860
1969	98,012	9,920	23,410
1970	98,935	10,580	23,900
1971	100,392	10,880	**
1972	103,976	11,545	**
1973	108,268	12,485	**
1974	108,854	13,335	**

Year	Government-Administered Plans		
	Railroad Retirement	Federal Civilian Employees	State and Local Employees
1930	1,400	432	800
1935	950	483	1,000
1940	1,349	745	1,552
1945	1,846	2,928	2,008
1950	1,881	1,873	2,894
1955	1,876	2,333	3,927
1960	1,654	2,707	5,160
1965	1,661	3,114	6,780
1966	1,666	3,322	7,210
1967	1,641	3,499	7,594
1968	1,625	3,565	8,012
1969	1,620	3,627	8,303
1970	1,633	3,625	8,591
1971	1,578	3,596	9,079
1972	1,575	3,737	9,563
1973	1,582	4,030	10,050
1974	1,592*	4,057*	10,845*

*Estimated.   ** Not available.

Sources: Railroad Retirement Board, Social Security Administration, Institute of Life Insurance

for the same dollar input because they live longer than men. Depending upon the annuity chosen, at age sixty-five, for each $1,000 a man will receive a life income of some $105 a year. The same sum will give a woman only about $86. If the annuity is purchased at age sixty-six, a man will be guaranteed about $107 annually; a woman will receive about $88. Each older age shows a corresponding higher return for both men and women. At age seventy, an annuity purchased for $1,000 will produce approximately $114 a year for a man and about $100 for a woman.

This type of annuity, a *life annuity*, ceases with the last payment preceding death. This annuity makes it possible to guarantee a comparatively high income for life regardless of how many years the annuitant survives. For it is evident that some annuitants will live long enough to receive considerably more money than they paid for their contracts. Thus, if a man were to purchase an annuity at age sixty-five for $10,000, he would receive some $1,050 each year for life. If he lives to eighty-five, he will have received some $21,000. These payments have actually been contributed to this long-lived annuitant by those who did not survive long enough to receive in benefits the money they paid for their contracts.

You may not think much of your chances of living to eighty-five. Quite reasonably, you could ask how long your $10,000 would last if you deposited it at 5 percent interest and withdrew $1,050 each year—the amount you could get from an annuity contract. Your $10,000 under such a "self-pension" plan would last over nineteen years. If you embarked on this program at sixty-five, you would do as well as you could with an annuity even if you lived to eighty-five. If you did not make it to this rather ripe old age, you would have done better outside the insurance company annuity, since at your death at any time prior to age eighty-five some portion of the principal you started with at sixty-five would still be intact.

Against this picture, you should weigh the possibility that you might live beyond eighty-five, and that investing in the annuity does serve to put the principal out of reach.

Inflation affects annuity's value

Inflation is a complex phenomenon and there is little agree-

Ups and Downs of Monthly Income
From a Variable Annuity*
(At Quarterly Intervals)

Date	Income For Month	Date	Income For Month
Nov. 1954	$100.00	Feb. 1964	$169.65
Feb. 1955	113.70	May	184.82
May	117.78	Aug.	188.88
Aug.	122.35	Nov.	204.62
Nov.	119.20	Feb. 1965	203.43
Feb. 1956	125.62	May	218.72
May	133.17	Aug.	207.45
Aug.	124.26	Nov.	233.89
Nov.	123.85	Feb. 1966	262.36
Feb. 1957	129.71	May	266.03
May	123.73	Aug.	240.11
Aug.	126.04	Nov.	213.68
Nov.	105.72	Feb. 1967	239.37
Feb. 1958	91.76	May	251.42
May	100.79	Aug.	273.61
Aug.	111.85	Nov.	272.10
Nov.	124.97	Feb. 1968	282.01
Feb. 1959	138.37	May	273.12
May	146.58	Aug.	288.96
Aug.	151.90	Nov.	311.15
Nov.	140.54	Feb. 1969	320.95
Feb. 1960	148.11	May	309.25
May	132.51	Aug.	279.14
Aug.	129.16	Nov.	274.71
Nov.	127.18	Feb. 1970	244.42
Feb. 1961	132.59	May	232.58
May	148.29	Aug.	204.67
Aug.	149.27	Nov.	222.82
Nov.	149.50	Feb. 1971	250.60
Feb. 1962	159.19	May	273.64
May	157.52	Aug.	268.10
Aug.	131.86	Nov.	267.25
Nov.	130.95	Feb. 1972	281.73
Feb. 1963	145.28	May	296.53
May	156.54	Aug.	274.15
Aug.	165.22	Nov.	273.15
Nov.	165.26	Feb. 1973	289.04
		May	259.58

* Contract issued by Aetna Variable Annuity Life Insurance Company.

ment even among the experts on its causes and cures. But most of them forecast continual shrinkage in the purchasing power of the dollar. In this light, the value of the life annuity becomes problematic. For while the income to be anticipated is assured and guaranteed to last as long as you live, there is the almost certain prospect that the purchasing power of the dollars you receive will continue to erode over the years.

If you do find yourself needing to stretch a sum of money to produce maximum income over a lifetime, you might give careful consideration to the *variable annuity*. Although the variable annuity has been made available to the general public for some twenty years, it is still relatively unknown to most people and to large sectors of the insurance sales force of the country. A life insurance agent cannot sell this annuity under his regular license issued by the insurance department of his state. He requires a separate license, for which he must take a special examination.

The basic difference between the life annuity and the variable annuity is that the former promises a stated fixed income while the latter provides an income which varies with the gains or losses of the insurance company's account for this type of contract. Since the company does not commit itself to any fixed return, it can invest the money it collects from the annuitants in common stocks, with the hope that such investments will provide a hedge against inflation. The number of units which are purchased by the annuitant are fixed throughout his lifetime but the value of the units fluctuates daily, depending on the rise or fall of the securities underlying the contracts.

By way of illustration, the table on page 147 sets forth the monthly variable annuity payments (at quarterly intervals) beginning in November, 1954, when the Aetna Variable Annuity Life Insurance Company (formerly Participating Annuity Life Insurance Company) issued the first variable annuity contract offered by a commercial insurance company to the general public.

There are several periods during which the annuity payments shown in the table decreased despite the fact that prices were rising (see the high point in February, 1969, which has not been equaled since, despite the sharp increase recorded in the cost of living during this same period). But it is also clear that the annuitant under this program fared better in the long run than he would have had he purchased a fixed annuity paying $100 a month for life. There is, of course, no assurance under the variable annuity that the payments will not decrease, while the fixed annuity payments would be guaranteed not to vary throughout the lifetime of the annuitant.

12

Choosing the Right Annuity

Most insurance companies that sell annuity contracts purchased at the point of retirement by one payment also offer a contract which is paid for by annual premiums. These plans can be purchased at any age to provide a life income at a later date. The age at which the retirement income is to begin usually is not specified in these contracts. You can elect to retire at any age after fifty or fifty-five, and the amount of income you will receive depends on the retirement age you select.

Thus, at age thirty-five you can purchase an annual premium retirement annuity on which you pay a premium of $100 each year. Twenty years later, when you are fifty-five, you can elect to receive an income of about $15 a month for as long as you live. You have the choice, however, of continuing the payment of the annual premium of $100 for the next ten years and can then, at the age of sixty-five, receive an income of about $35 a month for life.

The annual premium retirement annuity is really not an annuity at the time you purchase it. It is only at your retirement age that the total you have paid, plus interest and minus expenses, is applied to the purchase of an annuity. Prior to that time, your contract is actually a savings account into which you make regular deposits.

Annuity and savings plan compared

In itself, there is nothing wrong with making regular deposits into an annuity fund for future retirement. A program of this kind will serve to fix the return which can be expected at retirement, a factor which may prove valuable if life expectancies show a substantial improvement and annuity returns are reduced. But there are advantages in handling such funds outside of an insurance company.

The table on page 152 compares the cash available in a $100 annual premium retirement annuity with funds accumulated by depositing an equal amount of money each year in a savings or investment program earning 5 percent interest. The table shows that the fund accumulated in a straight savings plan will outstrip the cash values in the annual premium retirement annuity.

Since a retirement contract of this kind is not really an annuity during the accumulation period, it hardly seems wise to make payments into such a program.

The annual premium retirement annuity provides that in the event of death before the retirement age the premiums paid will be returned to the beneficiary. If the cash value is greater than the premiums paid, as it is in most companies after ten or eleven years, the cash value is paid. A straight savings account will provide more protection for dependents since the full deposits *plus interest* will be available to a beneficiary if the depositor should die.

If over the years you are able to set aside regular sums for your old age, you will be free to apply such funds to the purchase of an annuity when you retire. This procedure is precisely the one the insurance company follows in an annual premium retirement annuity.

Comparison of Annuity and Savings Fund

End of Year	Cash Available In Annuity With $100 Annual Premium*	Cash Available in Straight Savings By Depositing $100 per Year at 5% Interest Compounded Annually
1	$ 60	$ 105
2	151	215
3	247	331
4	343	453
5	446	580
10	993	1,321
15	1,600	2,266
20	2,366	3,472
25	3,221	5,011
30	4,212	6,976

* Annuity purchased at age 35 pays about $15 monthly for life beginning at age 55 or about $35 monthly for life beginning at age 65.

Note: All figures to the nearest dollar.

Certain features of the annual premium retirement annuity may be held up as being superior to accumulating retirement funds outside of an insurance company. Thus, if you purchase a retirement annuity today on an annual basis, you will have the assurance at retirement of a definite monthly income which is guaranteed in the contract, since the retirement annuity contains a table setting forth the income you can receive at each retirement age. If, on the other hand, you accumulate your retirement funds in a straight savings plan and approach an insurance company at your retirement age for an annuity, you will receive an income based on rates then in effect. Those rates may be less advantageous to you than present guarantees.

Conjectures as to future returns should not outweigh the fact that a 5 percent interest rate shows a better accumulation than these annuity contracts, and that there are definite risks of loss if you find it necessary to withdraw from these plans before the retirement age.

Other types of annuities

Some companies also sell an annuity to begin at a later retirement age for which you pay a single sum instead of annual amounts. This contract is similar to the annual premium plan, except that you pay for the contract in a lump sum. Under a contract of this type, you could make a single payment of $1,000 at age thirty-five and begin to receive a monthly income beginning at age sixty-five.

The shortcomings observed in connection with annual premium retirement plans apply equally to the contract purchased by a single payment. This contract, like the annual premium plan, is a savings account which is held at interest to be applied years hence to the purchase of an annuity. As in the case of the annual premium retirement annuity, this type of accumulation in a single sum plan may prove less desirable than straight savings outside of an insurance company.

There are also special contracts purchased by annual payments or by a single payment which differ from the more common annuity plans. Under these contracts, the retirement age is deferred to some future date but the contracts do not grant any cash values and generally offer no death benefits at any time, even prior to the retirement age.

Contracts of this type are not savings accumulations before the retirement age as is the annual premium annuity. These contracts, usually called *deferred annuities,* are based on the annuity principle from the time they are purchased. They provide a larger retirement income than the annual premium retirement annuity.

Deferred annuities have a place in situations where people do not need to provide for dependents and are in a position to put aside sums of money to which they will never have access. Such situations are uncommon, and this deferred annuity plan is of value to relatively few individuals.

Annuity is not life insurance

An annuity contract is not a substitute for life insurance. Some of these contracts, such as the annual premium retirement annuity, do show a death benefit, but it is important that you do not confuse this benefit with life insurance protection. The death benefit at any time before the retirement income begins is equal only to the premiums paid or to the cash value if that is larger in any year. A straight savings account will provide at least as much protection because it, too, will pass to the beneficiary of a deceased depositor and it will also include interest to the date of death.

The death benefits in an annuity do not place these contracts in the field of life insurance. Annuities, it is true, do not require a medical examination and may be purchased by persons who have been rejected for life insurance. But this is due precisely to the fact that there is no real element of life insurance risk to the company.

The annuity is actually the direct opposite of life insurance, for it protects against "living too long" while life insurance protects against "dying too soon." It cannot be emphasized too strongly that life insurance and annuities fill distinctly different functions.

You will do well to consider your needs for life insurance along the lines discussed in the first part of this book. If your death would cause financial loss to your family, you may be interested in creating an estate to protect your beneficiaries. Life insurance may have a definite place in such provisions. But annuities, even of the refund type, do not offer an answer to a need for life insurance. If an annuity is suggested as a replacement when you have been rejected for life insurance, you should understand that such a substitution is misleading.

Refund annuities

Several varieties of *refund annuities* are offered in which the full purchase price of the contract is guaranteed. If the annuitant does not live long enough to receive at least the amount he paid for the annuity, his beneficiary will receive the balance. As can be expected, the rates charged for refund annuities are higher than for the straight life annuity which ceases with the death of the annuitant regardless of when this takes place.

Thus, if in place of a life annuity purchased at age sixty-five for $10,000, a man chooses an *installment refund annuity*, he will receive only about $880 annually instead of about $1,050. The difference in return is even sharper in annuities purchased at older ages. At age seventy, a life annuity of $1,140 would be provided by $10,000 while only about $890 is offered on the cash refund basis for the same amount of money.

Since an annuity should be purchased primarily to obtain the highest possible income for life from the capital paid in, the refund type of contract defeats the basic purpose of the annuity because it provides a substantially lower income. There is no "loss" under the straight life annuity, even though payments cease at death, for it is precisely the spread of risk over large groups, benefiting those who live longer at the expense of those who die earlier, that makes up the annuity.

The refund annuity is often considered more desirable because it allows for some guaranteed income to a dependent. A married man who purchases an annuity at age sixty-five which will be continued throughout his life may prefer to take a smaller return but have this income continued for his widow after his death. This type of guarantee in the refund annuity offers only a very limited answer to the old-age needs of his dependent wife since it will not continue throughout her life but will cease when the original purchase price of the contract has been paid. It would be better where two aged lives are involved to purchase an annuity covering both lives.

Joint and survivor annuities

Annuities are offered which guarantee an income throughout the joint lives of two persons and continue this income to the survivor as long as he or she lives. The returns under such contracts are smaller than under a single life annuity, but *joint and survivor annuities* fill a definite need in the retirement plans of an aged couple because such contracts stretch funds to the maximum for both lives.

Most companies writing annuities will issue these joint and survivor contracts. Some companies offer a slightly higher income while both annuitants are alive, to be followed by a reduced income to the survivor. Usually, contracts of this type are written to continue two-thirds of the income after the death of the first annuitant, and are called *joint and two-*

thirds to survivor annuities. Many persons prefer this type of arrangement, for it permits a larger income when both annuitants are alive, with sufficient income for the reduced needs of one survivor.

You may prefer the higher returns of a joint and two-thirds to survivor annuity during the lifetimes of both annuitants even though a reduced income is payable to the survivor. The company from which you wish to purchase a contract on two lives may offer only the joint and survivor annuity which is not reduced after the death of the first annuitant. You can try to obtain the annuity elsewhere or, by employing the following method, you can arrange in such a company for an annuity similar to the joint and two-thirds to survivor contract.

When you apply for the annuity, inform the company that you wish to purchase three separate contracts. One is to be written on your life, one will cover your wife, and the third will be written on the joint and survivor plan. The income to be produced under each of these annuities is to be the same. Thus, if each of the three contracts provides $100 a month, you and your wife receive $300 a month from these annuity contracts during your joint lives. The survivor will receive income from only two of these contracts—the one on his own life and the joint and survivor plan. The income will then continue at the rate of $200 a month throughout the lifetime of the survivor. In this way, you will have provided a joint and two-thirds to survivor annuity.

This same procedure can be used to achieve any other combination providing for a different percentage of income to the survivor. You might feel that your needs will be served best by a *joint and three-quarters to survivor annuity.* By following the technique outlined, you can arrange for such a share to be paid to the survivor.

If you feel that only one-half of the income will be needed by the survivor, you can purchase two joint annuities for yourself and your wife, each providing an equal income. The survivor under such an arrangement will receive half of the annuity income which was paid while both annuitants were alive.

Homeowner and Tenant Protection

CHAPTER 13

Fire Coverage for Your Home

Increasingly in recent years, insurance on private dwellings and their contents is being purchased under special Homeowners policies which package coverage on the house, the contents, and the liability of the insured person and members of his household. Apartment dwellers also have available to them a Homeowners policy which covers the contents of the apartment and the liability of the householder.

These Homeowners policies are described on pages 225-230. In this and the next five chapters we shall analyze each group of perils separately so that the various types of coverage can be easily understood and adapted to individual needs and preferences. There are some situations in which separate fire insurance is still necessary, as when a dwelling is not owner-occupied, and for this type of homeowner the analysis of the separate coverages should be particularly helpful.

As in all property insurance, the first step in a program of proper protection against fire calls for an accurate determination of the value of the property to be covered.

Too often, the amount of fire insurance on a home is found to be inadequate only after the property has been damaged or destroyed, and the homeowner suffers severe loss. Conversely, carrying more insurance than is required by the value of the property is a waste of money.

To guard against the pitfalls of inadequate or improper insurance as well as the waste of overinsurance, it is essential that you establish with reasonable accuracy the actual value of your property.

Furthermore, in order to translate the value of your property into a correct insurance figure, you should have some understanding of the practical applications of the policy's provisions and the protection it affords.

"Actual cash value"

Your fire insurance policy insures your property to the extent of the "actual cash value" but "not exceeding the amount which it would cost to repair or replace the damage done." Definitions and interpretations of "actual cash value" occupy a very considerable place in the legal decisions of the various states, and the precise meaning of this phrase can often be decided in a particular case only at the time of the actual loss.

It has been held that "actual cash value" is not the equivalent of the market value of the property, or what it cost originally, or what it would cost to rebuild at the time of a loss, but rather the utility of the property to its owner.

Most of the complexities that surround this question apply to commercial buildings and merchandise held for sale, and do not ordinarily affect residences too severely. We can feel reasonably safe if we guide ourselves by the cost to repair, rebuild, or replace the property lost or damaged with another of similar kind and quality.

In figuring the cost of replacement of damaged property, the insurance company will take into account the depreciation that has taken place in the property since it was first erected. In arriving at a correct figure for your insurance, you must base it on the present condition of the property. Changes in

Coverage Against Fire
And Other Perils

Despite the popularity of homeowner and commercial "package" policies, the amount of separate coverage against fire and other perils has increased, as shown in this table of premiums paid for the years 1948 through 1974.

Year	Fire	Allied Perils*
1948	$1,292,788,000	$ 321,214,000
1949	1,328,391,000	345,357,000
1950	1,407,857,000	378,283,000
1951	1,503,579,000	453,762,000
1952	1,506,946,000	508,493,000
1953	1,534,379,000	547,807,000
1954	1,545,894,000	595,984,000
1955	1,560,549,000	677,381,000
1956	1,582,563,000	714,606,000
1957	1,593,996,000	712,460,000
1958	1,626,167,000	766,596,000
1959	1,709,257,000	779,583,000
1960	1,667,385,000	738,910,000
1961	1,619,076,000	709,530,000
1962	1,623,046,000	715,518,000
1963	1,571,957,000	698,697,000
1964	1,533,481,000	678,117,000
1965	1,548,139,000	667,254,000
1966	1,605,668,000	675,603,000
1967	1,681,963,000	704,604,000
1968	1,827,169,000	751,223,000
1969	2,017,465,000	856,766,000
1970	2,199,424,000	947,958,000
1971	2,293,693,000	878,543,000
1972	2,463,217,000	942,452,000
1973	2,392,078,000	1,025,042,000
1974	2,350,000,000	1,150,000,000

*Covers a wide variety of perils, including windstorm, riot, explosion, sprinkler leakage, water damage, and earthquake.

Sources: *Best's Aggregates & Averages*, Insurance Information Institute

real estate values, improvements made since the time of construction, alterations, and additions will all figure in the final estimate of the present value of your property.

Two special forms for insuring private dwellings which broaden the coverage to include a series of perils beyond the basic fire policy also permit insuring on a replacement basis rather than on an "actual cash value" basis. These special dwelling policies will be discussed in the chapter that follows. Replacement cost coverage is also part of the Homeowners package policies to be discussed later. Where such replacement cost coverage is afforded, there will be no deduction for depreciation in the settlement of any loss to the dwelling property, provided the amount of insurance is adequate.

Appraisal of property

Construction costs have changed so drastically within recent years that many homeowners find it a wise practice to have a competent builder appraise the present value of their structure. Often, an insurance company representative who is familiar with property values can be called upon to help you estimate the present value of your home.

Where such physical appraisal of the property is not practical, it may help if you consult one of the published guides to construction costs which will show you how much values have risen on the average over the years since you acquired your home. Your insurance agent or company can usually supply you with a guide of this kind.

In addition to the value of the building itself, you should include all materials and equipment used in the maintenance of the building, such as hoses and other fire-extinguishing apparatus, floor coverings and furnishings of corridors and stairs, window shades, awnings, screens, storm doors, and so forth.

All additions and extensions to the building which are structurally attached, all improvements, and all permanent fixtures, such as walks, yard fixtures, and fences, are to be taken into account in arriving at the total value of the property.

Trees, plants, and shrubbery are usually outside the coverage of the regular policy, and call for separate insurance.

There is limited insurance, however, on such property under the broader forms of coverage for private dwellings and under the Homeowners package policies.

Policies on dwellings also afford an additional amount of insurance, equal to 10 percent of the coverage on the dwelling itself, to cover other private structures located on the premises. Where the insurance on the main residential building is sufficient, it will usually cover the garage and other outbuildings. Thus, if you carry $30,000 of insurance on your home, you will not need to provide specific insurance on outbuildings unless their value exceeds $3,000.

In arriving at a figure for the actual cash value of your property, you should omit all your household and personal effects as well as all such property belonging to any member, guest, or servant of your household. Insurance on personal effects is provided as a separate item in policies covering dwellings as well as under the Homeowners package policies.

What the fire policy covers

Before you decide on the size of your fire insurance policy, you should be clear on the protection the contract affords. The policy will indemnify not only for fire losses but also for damage from smoke, cracking, and blistering from heat of the fire. Water damage and other losses brought about in the process of extinguishing the blaze are also recoverable, as is loss caused by removal of property from premises endangered by fire.

The fire policy also covers direct loss by lightning, even when no fire ensues, and the destruction of the property ordered by any civil authority to prevent the spread of fire.

It is strongly recommended that your fire insurance cover at least 80 percent of the full value of your property. It is true that the chances of total loss are relatively slight, at least in areas within easy reach of efficient fire-fighting equipment. But even in such areas, there is always some possibility of a total or near-total loss from fire, lightning, or the allied perils that come within the range of fire insurance. And it is precisely the catastrophic loss, less likely though it is, that can least be borne by the individual and should be shifted to the insuring company.

Where Fires Occur
Percentage of Total Dollar Loss

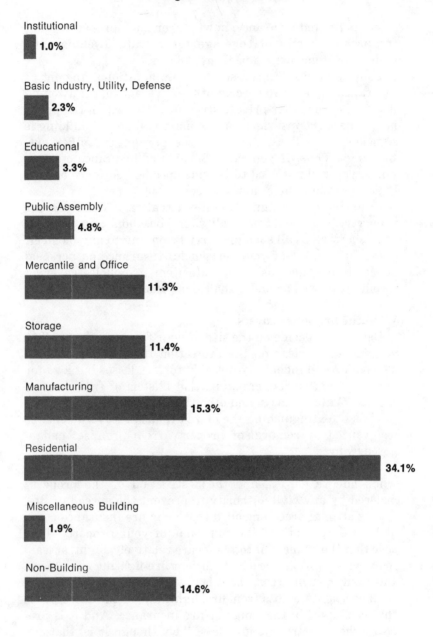

Institutional
1.0%

Basic Industry, Utility, Defense
2.3%

Educational
3.3%

Public Assembly
4.8%

Mercantile and Office
11.3%

Storage
11.4%

Manufacturing
15.3%

Residential
34.1%

Miscellaneous Building
1.9%

Non-Building
14.6%

Sources: National Fire Protection Association estimates for 1974, Insurance Information Institute

Caution necessary

Even if you would feel content with less than 80 percent insurance on your property's value, it is extremely important that you determine whether this procedure is permitted by the terms of your policy. In the populous areas of New York State (and optionally in certain other areas) inadequate insurance will definitely prove costly to the policyholder when his property is damaged by any of the perils insured in the contract.

Fire insurance policies and Homeowners package policies in New York may include a special clause which in effect controls the amount of insurance you must carry if you would collect in full on any loss. Basically, the clause is an agreement that the insured person will carry a certain amount of insurance in proportion to the value of his property. The most common stipulation is that the total insurance will not be less than 80 percent of the value of the property covered.

This does not mean that the company will insist on your buying any definite amount of insurance. Usually, the figure you set for your fire insurance will be accepted by the company and a policy will be issued in any amount you order. The question of the adequacy of your insurance may arise only when you suffer a loss which is covered by the policy.

In the state of New York, if your policy contains a coinsurance clause, known to you or not, and you do not carry sufficient insurance, you will collect only a percentage of any loss you suffer, regardless of the size of your loss.

Let us assume your home is situated within easy reach of a fire department and you feel quite confident that any fire at your premises will be brought under control before a total loss is incurred. Your home is worth $40,000 and you carry $24,000 of fire insurance in a policy which contains an 80 percent coinsurance clause. When a fire does actually break out at your home, it is extinguished before it has damaged more than $3,000 of your property. You feel secure with your $24,000 insurance policy but discover when the loss is adjusted that the company's liability is limited to 75 percent of the loss. To meet the terms of this policy with its coinsurance clause, the company pays you $2,250 as settlement of the $3,000 loss you incurred.

The percentage of loss for which the company is liable is determined by the ratio of the total insurance to 80 percent of the actual cash value of the property. In this case, where your home was worth $40,000, you should have carried at least $32,000 of insurance—80 percent of $40,000. Since the total insurance on the property was only $24,000, the company's liability is limited to the ratio of this $24,000 to the $32,000 of insurance you were required to carry—or 75 percent. The proportion is expressed as follows:

$$\frac{\$24,000 \text{ (amount of insurance carried)}}{\$32,000 \text{ (80 percent of actual cash value of property)}} = \frac{3}{4} \text{ or 75 percent}$$

This percentage will be used by the company in adjusting any loss you suffer. If the damage inflicted by the fire were, for example, $10,000, you would receive 75 percent of this amount, $7,500.

When your insurance is not large enough to fulfill the coinsurance requirements of the policy, you act as a partial insurer. The company carries part of the risk, and you carry the balance.

Carry adequate insurance

It is important to bear in mind that the coinsurance clause contains the words "at the time the loss should happen." This means that the amount of insurance you carry must comply with the 80 percent provision at the time the loss occurs, not at the time you acquired the policy. It is consequently no defense to show that the insurance was adequate in relation to the value of the property at the time you bought the policy. All additions and improvements as well as any increase in the value of the property since the policy was purchased will be taken into account in deciding whether you have met the coinsurance requirements of the policy.

This factor is especially important today when building costs and real estate values have risen so precipitously. Whether or not your policy contains a coinsurance clause, you should make sure that the amount of insurance you are carrying is adequate in view of existing costs, and not in relation to the values which prevailed when you first insured your home.

The coinsurance clause is not incorporated into policies on residential property located in states other than New York. Under policies written without coinsurance clauses, no set amount of insurance is required. The company will pay the full amount of any loss up to the limits of the policy. Carrying insufficient insurance in such cases will, of course, still result in drastic loss to a homeowner if the loss exceeds the amount of insurance maintained. Adequate insurance protection is therefore certainly indicated even though no coinsurance requirements are specified.

In some parts of New York State, the homeowner may be offered a policy either with or without a coinsurance clause. A reduction in rate is granted where the policy includes this feature. If you are adequately insured and your policy covers 80 percent of your property's value, you should have your policy written with a coinsurance clause. In this way, you will receive the lower rate granted for such policies.

Unoccupied houses

Most fire policy forms now allow for the insured premises to be vacant or unoccupied for sixty consecutive days. In areas which are within close reach of fire hydrants and fire-fighting equipment unlimited unoccupancy is usually permitted by the terms of the policy. A few contracts limit such periods to ten days. The policy does not cover any loss which occurs in premises unoccupied after the period permitted.

Where a building is used only as a summer or seasonal dwelling, a special form may be necessary to allow for longer unoccupancy. You should check the insurance you carry on such seasonal property to make sure the premises may be unoccupied for long periods.

If you had previously occupied your home on a year-round basis and now plan to use the premises only during certain seasons, you should notify the insurance company of this fact so that the policy may be properly endorsed. If you close your home for any protracted period, similar notification should be given the company. The rate for insurance which allows for longer periods of unoccupancy may be a little higher, but your policy must be appropriately endorsed if you are to avoid complete loss of protection during such periods.

A contrary situation to the one just outlined might arise at your home. You may decide to reside permanently in the house you had formerly used only seasonally, or you may for the first time rent your summer residence to a tenant for the winter months. In such a case, where your home is occupied steadily by yourself or a tenant, you no longer require special seasonal dwelling forms. The ordinary unoccupancy periods of the regular policy will be ample for your changed situation. You should therefore have the policy corrected to take into account the year-round occupancy of the insured premises. A lower rate is usually granted on such forms and you can take advantage of the saving in premium from the time when the premises are occupied either by yourself or by a tenant.

It is likely that your fire insurance policy grants you the right to make alterations and repairs. If you are in doubt on this point and are planning alterations of an extensive nature, it is best that you inform the insurance company of your plans. In this way, there will be no question of your having breached your policy, which incorporates a condition that the insurance will be "suspended while the hazard is increased within the knowledge or control of the insured."

Buying multiple insurance

An important rule to follow where more than one policy covers the same property is that all such policies be written alike. The description of the property, the policy forms, and special endorsements should be identical in all policies. The coinsurance clauses in the policies should be similar too. This precaution may avoid difficulty when a loss is being settled.

Most policy forms now provide insurance on your interest in property purchased on the installment plan. If you have any sizable amount of property or equipment of which you are not the sole owner, check your insurance to make sure that your interest in this property is covered. If your property carries a mortgage, the policy may be written to cover the mortgagee's interest as well as your own.

Most persons who build a house hire a contractor or builder, who usually provides insurance on the materials and the building in process of construction. If you plan to build a home without engaging a contractor, you will require a spe-

Fire Losses in the United States

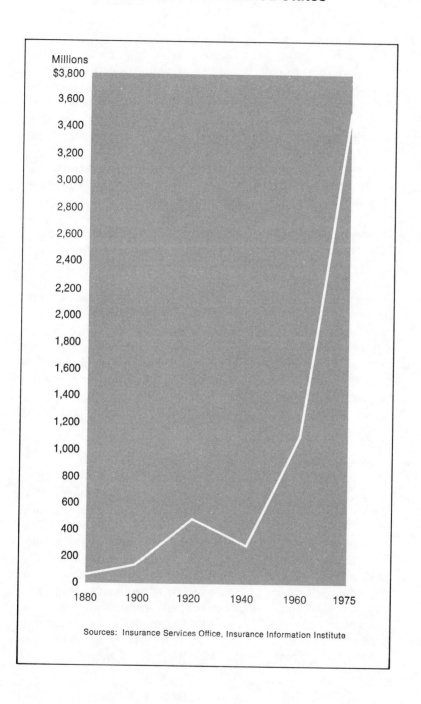

Sources: Insurance Services Office, Insurance Information Institute

cial policy to cover the structure as it is being erected.

It can be helpful when erecting a new building or remodeling an old one to get the advice of your insurance agent or company representative. He can often suggest improved methods and materials which may cost a little more but will result in lower insurance premiums. In the long run, these savings may amortize the extra cost of the superior construction.

If you purchase a home on which fire insurance is current, be sure that the company is notified of the change in ownership of the insured property. Formerly, a policy was void if any change, other than the death of the insured, took place in the interest, title, or possession of the insured property. Most policies being written today have eliminated this restriction, but no assignment of the policy is valid except with the written consent of the company.

In case of a loss, you should give immediate notice to the insurance company or its representative, preferably in writing. Despite the widespread impression to the contrary, it is not necessary to leave the property undisturbed until the company's representative arrives. It is in fact a strict requirement that you take immediate steps to save and preserve the property from further damage. The damaged property should be separated from undamaged property, and every reasonable effort made to prevent any further loss.

Saving on premium

Rates for fire insurance are regulated closely by the state authorities and there has been considerable standardization among most of the companies doing business in any jurisdiction. There is a growing trend toward more competition among companies, and some states now have "open rating" laws under which companies are permitted relative freedom in establishing rates. It would therefore be advisable to check the rate you are being charged against those offered by other companies—whether stock or mutual. Additionally, there are numerous "direct writers" which deal with the public only through their own full-time representatives (for example, Allstate and State Farm) and their rates might offer you economies.

No one kind of company can be counted on to offer all forms of insurance at the lowest rates, and only actual comparison in your individual situation can reveal the best values.

It should be emphasized that a relationship of mutual confidence with an agent is a valuable asset which is not to be discarded lightly in favor of the saving of a few dollars when a policy is written. Insurance is a promise to pay at some unknown date, and sound advice and service throughout the life of a policy must be weighed into the scale of costs.

Mutual companies

When seeking fire insurance you should bear in mind that a mutual company is subject to regulation by the same state insurance department which sets standards for reserves of all companies within its jurisdiction. The mutual company, even as the stock company, must comply with certain requirements for dispersion and limitation of its individual risks, must provide for reinsurance against unexpected "catastrophe" losses, and must abide by circumscribed investment possibilities.

A mutual company will approach its insuring activities with much the same safeguards as any other company in its state. These safeguards reduce the possibility that a company will need to levy assessments on policyholders. There are many mutual companies which have retained the right to assess their policyholders throughout a century or more of activity but have never exercised this right.

It is possible to buy insurance in mutual companies which do not have the right to assess policyholders. There are many mutual organizations with high comparative ratings which issue policies that are explicitly nonassessable.

If you do buy your insurance from a mutual company, its policies should exclude the right of assessment. It is fairly simple to check whether a particular company issues nonassessable policies by reading what should be clearly stamped on the policy. If you have any doubts on this score, ask an agent of the company or write to your state insurance department for the information you require.

You need not restrict yourself to companies of any particular class—stock, mutual, cooperatives, direct writers. You should, however, stand firm on the conditions that a company should fulfill:

1. It should write at favorable rates or, if it charges "standard" rates but returns dividends to its policyholders, it should have a fairly consistent record of such dividend distributions. A dividend of about 15 percent of the premium may be anticipated on fire insurance policies.

2. It should be considered favorably by your state insurance department. This public agency will furnish without charge an appraisal of any company that operates in the state. You could also ask to have the company checked in an accepted insurance rating publication, such as *Best's Insurance Guide*.

A basic policy insuring your property against fire may be all the coverage you believe is necessary. However, there are many other hazards which might damage or destroy your home. These perils and the coverage available to protect you against them are discussed in the next chapter.

CHAPTER 14

Coverage for Windstorm and Other Perils

Most homeowners who purchase fire insurance policies add coverage against windstorm losses under an endorsement which combines protection against a group of perils. These perils are all covered as well under each of the Homeowner package policies. This supplementary protection endorsement covers, subject to policy provisions, the perils of:

- windstorm and hail
- explosion
- riot, riot attending a strike, and civil commotion
- aircraft and vehicles
- smoke

Of these additional coverages, the windstorm group is the most important, and this more inclusive endorsement is usually added to the policy primarily for its insurance against these perils.

The Hurricane Record
(1925-1974)

A total of 5,046 persons have died in the 87 hurricanes that have reached the continental United States during the past 5 decades.

Year	Hurricanes	Deaths*	Year	Hurricanes	Deaths*
1924	2	2	1950	3	19
1925	1	6	1951	0	0
1926	4	269	1952	1	3
1927	0	0	1953	2	2
1928	2	1,836	1954	3	193
1929	2	3	1955	3	218
1930	0	0	1956	1	21
1931	0	0	1957	1	395
1932	2	0	1958	0	2
1933	5	63	1959	3	24
1934	3	17	1960	2	65
1935	2	414	1961	1	46
1936	3	9	1962	0	4
1937	0	0	1963	1	11
1938	2	600	1964	4	49
1939	1	3	1965	1	75
1940	2	51	1966	2	54
1941	2	10	1967	1	18
1942	2	8	1968	1	9
1943	1	16	1969	2	256
1944	3	64	1970	1	11
1945	3	7	1971	3	8
1946	1	0	1972	1	121
1947	3	53	1973	0	5
1948	3	3	1974	1	1
1949	2	4			

*Include fatalities from high winds of less than hurricane force.

Sources: National Oceanic and Atmospheric Administration, Insurance Information Institute

The coverages provided under the riot portion of the extended coverage endorsement are self-explanatory. There are questions in some instances of whether damage to insured property was a result of a riot, a term which is defined in the statutes of many states, although not always in the same way. A common law definition of riot states that it is "a tumultuous disturbance of the peace by three or more persons acting in concert." Civil commotion is not defined as such but a court has held that "an aggravated riot may, if prolonged, become a civil commotion."

While damage by an object falling from an aircraft is covered, the vehicles provision requires that there be actual physical contact of a vehicle with the property. Thus, if a truck were to cause a stone to fly and break a window of your home, there would be no extended coverage protection for this loss.

The endorsement assumes liability for damage to insured property inflicted by vehicles running on land or tracks. No insurance is provided against damage from any vehicle owned or operated by the insured person or his tenants. Also excluded from the policy is all damage to fences, driveways, walks, or lawns.

The smoke and explosion clauses of the extended coverage endorsement further broaden the insurance against these perils provided in the regular fire insurance policy.

"Hostile" and "friendly" fires

Under the fire insurance itself, smoke damage or explosion caused by fire is covered, but only when the fire is "hostile." A hostile fire may be defined roughly as one which is outside its proper place. A fire which stays within a furnace or other cooking or heating apparatus is a "friendly" fire and smoke damage from such cause is not covered under the regular fire policy.

The extended coverage endorsement broadens the scope of the insurance to include almost any smoke damage from an ordinary heating or cooking unit in use on the premises. Smoke from fireplaces is excepted, and in some states only stoves connected to a chimney by a smoke pipe come within the insuring clause of the endorsement.

Tornadoes by State

Tornadoes struck at least once in every state except Alaska during the 1970-74 period, causing 704 deaths and 14,573 injuries. The South and the Midwest are hit most often by tornadoes.

Five-Year Totals, 1970-74

State	Tornadoes	Deaths	Injuries
Alabama	134	96	1,544
Alaska	0	0	0
Arizona	39	1	111
Arkansas	109	10	607
California	12	0	1
Colorado	55	0	17
Connecticut	16	0	2
Delaware	1	0	0
District of Columbia	0	0	0
Florida	283	3	408
Georgia	170	27	480
Hawaii	6	0	4
Idaho	4	0	0
Illinois	233	8	209
Indiana	118	48	950
Iowa	138	6	175
Kansas	200	12	325
Kentucky	88	81	1,507
Louisiana	137	17	241
Maine	19	0	2
Maryland	12	0	4
Massachusetts	26	6	58
Michigan	100	3	68
Minnesota	75	1	42
Mississippi	183	125	1,954
Missouri	175	11	306
Montana	15	0	0

Five-Year Totals, 1970-74

State	Tornadoes	Deaths	Injuries
Nebraska	147	0	35
Nevada	5	0	1
New Hampshire	15	0	7
New Jersey	45	0	12
New Mexico	49	1	9
New York	27	2	14
North Carolina	70	10	188
North Dakota	73	0	18
Ohio	114	47	1,570
Oklahoma	239	39	700
Oregon	5	0	0
Pennsylvania	36	1	24
Rhode Island	1	0	0
South Carolina	44	16	124
South Dakota	151	1	20
Tennessee	109	51	1,106
Texas	719	70	1,238
Utah	6	0	1
Vermont	5	0	7
Virginia	23	1	63
Washington	9	6	301
West Virginia	13	1	34
Wisconsin	113	3	86
Wyoming	26	0	0
Puerto Rico	4	0	0
Countrywide Total	4,332*	704	14,573

*Corrected for boundary-crossing tornadoes.

Sources: National Oceanic and Atmospheric Administration, Insurance Information Institute

The same widening of coverage applies to explosion losses. Under the fire policy, if a fire causes an explosion, the entire loss would be covered, but no other explosion damage is considered. The endorsement includes the peril of explosion and covers any occurrence of this kind except those of steam boilers, steam pipes, steam turbines, steam engines, and machinery connected with them.

Most loss or damage caused by wind, cyclone, or tornado is covered under this endorsement, although certain property and conditions are specifically excluded. Thus, the company is not liable for damage to buildings in process of construction or reconstruction unless the building is entirely enclosed under a roof, with all outside doors and windows permanently in place.

Damage or loss from rain or water is not covered even if driven by the wind, unless the wind first causes actual damage to the roof or walls and the rain enters the interior of the building through these openings. If the wind damages the walls or roof of the insured property and breaks pipes of a sprinkler or water system, the resultant water damage is covered. No coverage is granted on stacked grain, hay, or straw, nor on windmills, windpumps or their towers, unless specially added to the policy by the company.

The type of construction of your residence will, of course, affect the likelihood of a serious windstorm loss, as will the house's location. The hazards of windstorm, cyclone, and tornado show sharp variations in intensity in different sections of the country and also during certain months of the year. Experience with windstorm insurance has shown that states near the coastline generally have a higher degree of hazard, with Texas usually the heaviest sufferer.

Extended coverage for all policies

If you decide to add extended coverage to your fire insurance, it is essential that you include this supplementary coverage in all the fire insurance covering your property. You may feel that the windstorm hazard does not threaten your home with damage as complete as fire and may think it sufficient to add this coverage to only part of your insurance. Such a procedure is to be avoided as it will result in your re-

Insurance Provided by Beach and Windstorm Plans

| State | New Applications 1974 | Binders or Policies Issued 1974 | | Insurance In Force (000 omitted) |
		Original	Renewal	
Alabama	302	266	1,150	$ 28,531
Florida	4,409	3,307	10,252	642,629
Louisiana	1,367	5,572	*	94,065
Mississippi	882	804	6,536	148,572
North Carolina	582	451	3,082	82,407
South Carolina	631	599	1,561	80,422
Texas	52,497	43,024	*	1,064,772
Totals	60,670	54,023	22,581	$2,141,398

* Included with new applications.

Sources: Property Insurance Plans Service Office, Insurance Information Institute

ceiving only partial indemnity for any windstorm damage or other loss covered under this endorsement.

Thus, if you have two $20,000 fire insurance contracts covering your property and you add extended coverage to only one of these policies, you will receive only 50 percent indemnity for any loss covered under the extended coverage endorsement. Even if the windstorm or other loss you incur causes only $1,000 of damage, you can recover just $500 in this instance even though you carry $20,000 of windstorm protection in the extended coverage endorsement. The proportion of liability assumed by the company is based on the ratio of the extended coverage insurance to all fire insurance on the property.

A fire insurance policy to which the extended coverage endorsement has been added may be broadened further to cover the perils of vandalism and malicious mischief. The cost of this added protection is very low, usually about ten cents per $1,000 of insurance, and the homeowner should have this extra protection incorporated into his fire policy.

A fire policy with the extended coverage and vandalism and malicious mischief endorsements provides insurance against twelve distinct perils. (The Homeowners Form 1 policy covers all these perils as well as liability.) Two forms to cover private dwellings only are now offered, and each of these further broadens the coverage. The Dwelling Building and Contents Broad Form brings within the scope of the policy the additional perils of:

• sudden and accidental tearing asunder, cracking, burning, or bulging of a steam or hot water heating system and appliances for heating water for domestic consumption
• damage by burglars
• freezing of plumbing, heating, and air conditioning systems
• damage by falling objects
• collapse of building or any part thereof
• weight of ice, snow, or sleet
• breakage of glass
• damage to electrical appliances, fixtures, and wiring from artificially generated electrical currents
• smoke (almost any smoke damage is covered, but under the extended coverage endorsement the smoke must originate from heating or cooking units connected to a chimney)
• accidental discharge of water or steam from within plumbing, heating, or air conditioning systems or domestic appliances

The last listed peril causes numerous and often substantial losses, for in these situations it is frequently necessary to tear out and replace portions of the structure. The entire cost of such work is specifically assumed under this feature of the policy.

This considerably broadened coverage may be written not only on the dwelling but also on its contents. (The Homeowners Form 2 policy includes under its property sections all the perils listed above.)

Broader coverage available

Broader than the fire insurance policy with all the previously mentioned endorsements added (which would encom-

pass over twenty distinct perils) is the Dwelling Building
Special Form. This policy is available to cover private dwellings but not their contents. It is an all-risk policy which does
not list the perils covered but covers "all risks of direct
physical loss" except for the stated exclusions. Basically, the
excepted perils are those of wear, tear, and depreciation;
earthquake, volcanic eruption, and landslide; flood and rising
surface waters, waves, tidal waters, and the seepage of water
through sidewalks, foundations, walls, basement, or other
floors.

There are restrictions on the length of time during which a
dwelling unoccupied beyond four weeks will have coverage
against water losses if the policyholder has not maintained
heat in the structure or drained the water system. Certain
types of property also are specifically not covered but, by and
large, the policy affords extremely comprehensive protection
on dwelling property. (The Homeowers Form 3 policy covers
the dwelling itself on this same all-risk basis; the contents
are covered for the twenty specific perils listed under the
broad form policy. The Homeowners Form 5 policy provides
all-risk insurance on both building and contents.)

A valuable feature of the Dwelling Building Broad Form
and the Dwelling Building Special Form as well as all the
Homeowner package policies is the replacement cost coverage. All these policies permit the insured person to recover
the cost of repairs to his building (but not the contents) on
a replacement cost basis, i.e., without deduction for depreciation, if at the time of the loss the full amount of the insurance
is equal to 80 percent or more of the replacement cost of the
dwelling. If the amount of coverage is less than this percentage of the full replacement cost, the loss is settled on the basis
of the "actual cash value" of the property as discussed under
the fire insurance policy analysis in the preceding chapter.

Insurance against water hazards

None of the policies covering dwellings, even if on an all-
risk basis, extends to loss by flood, rising water, or tidal wave.
Property owners exposed to these hazards may be able to
procure insurance if the area in which their property is located has been designated as eligible by the Federal Insurance

Purchases of Flood Insurance Soar

The lessons taught by the catastrophic floods of mid-1972 are credited in part with the sharp subsequent increase in the purchase of flood insurance. Between May 31, 1972, and May 31, 1975, the number of policies in force increased from 92,590 to 511,000 and the dollar amount of insurance coverage soared from $1.48 billion to over $12.4 billion.

| State | No. of Communities | Policies in Force | | |
		Dwelling	Business and Other	Total
Alabama	124	2,545	1,022	3,567
Alaska	10	1,892	219	2,111
Arizona	48	8,138	720	8,858
Arkansas	134	2,015	655	2,670
California	249	12,481	2,548	15,029
Colorado	92	1,471	589	2,060
Connecticut	107	3,074	832	3,906
Delaware	33	1,757	490	2,247
Florida	250	87,650	11,937	99,587
Georgia	133	2,343	387	2,730
Hawaii	4	2,066	431	2,497
Idaho	66	502	51	553
Illinois	408	9,100	1,390	10,490
Indiana	174	1,090	310	1,400
Iowa	113	2,173	594	2,767
Kansas	106	1,003	406	1,409
Kentucky	103	1,824	791	2,615
Louisiana	181	83,719	9,724	93,443
Maine	273	510	189	699
Maryland	78	3,261	1,634	4,895
Massachusetts	159	4,666	1,821	6,487
Michigan	254	8,156	902	9,058
Minnesota	331	1,921	341	2,262

State	No. of Communities	Insurance in Force (000 omitted)		
		Dwelling	Business and Other	Total
Alabama	124	$53,142	$20,466	$73,608
Alaska	10	49,264	6,231	55,495
Arizona	48	175,603	11,395	186,998
Arkansas	134	31,881	10,812	42,693
California	249	335,555	54,409	389,964
Colorado	92	33,479	17,960	51,439
Connecticut	107	79,731	19,460	99,191
Delaware	33	51,408	14,423	65,831
Florida	250	2,496,623	392,069	2,888,692
Georgia	133	53,110	7,830	60,940
Hawaii	4	69,134	16,106	85,240
Idaho	66	10,385	762	11,147
Illinois	408	153,604	25,537	179,141
Indiana	174	20,199	5,814	26,013
Iowa	113	34,137	11,532	45,668
Kansas	106	15,138	7,253	22,391
Kentucky	103	30,330	12,187	42,517
Louisiana	181	2,145,710	206,150	2,351,860
Maine	273	9,665	3,541	13,206
Maryland	78	85,794	51,244	137,038
Massachusetts	159	102,876	39,913	142,789
Michigan	254	164,585	19,560	184,145
Minnesota	331	33,604	6,751	40,355

Purchases of Flood Insurance Soar *(Continued)*

State	No. of Communities	Policies in Force Dwelling	Policies in Force Business and Other	Total
Mississippi	182	14,698	3,096	17,794
Missouri	223	5,050	1,665	6,715
Montana	26	473	28	501
Nebraska	108	1,425	250	1,675
Nevada	9	545	17	562
New Hampshire	28	143	103	246
New Jersey	396	26,691	8,395	35,086
New Mexico	35	717	139	856
New York	533	16,907	3,673	20,580
North Carolina	160	5,674	2,876	8,550
North Dakota	50	2,731	324	3,055
Ohio	223	4,291	957	5,248
Oklahoma	85	3,742	796	4,538
Oregon	171	2,211	1,177	3,388
Pennsylvania	1,154	28,365	9,192	37,557
Puerto Rico	1	2,603	552	3,155
Rhode Island	30	2,498	1,513	4,011
South Carolina	78	5,783	1,771	7,554
South Dakota	43	640	231	871
Tennessee	127	1,278	510	1,788
Texas	350	43,477	7,483	50,960
Utah	74	177	20	197
Vermont	58	207	170	377
Virginia	206	5,346	1,722	7,068
Washington	152	2,216	434	2,651
West Virginia	135	1,120	534	1,654
Wisconsin	204	2,035	363	2,398
Wyoming	20	186	42	228
Countrywide	8,382	424,586	86,016	510,603

State	No. of Communities	Insurance in Force (000 omitted)		
		Dwelling	Business and Other	Total
Mississippi	182	$291,115	$60,662	$351,777
Missouri	223	78,727	29,180	107,907
Montana	26	10,097	623	10,720
Nebraska	108	28,805	6,226	35,031
Nevada	9	13,245	457	13,702
New Hampshire	28	2,614	2,784	5,398
New Jersey	396	762,148	231,217	993,365
New Mexico	35	17,274	2,885	20,159
New York	533	421,192	108,030	529,222
North Carolina	160	144,501	70,823	215,323
North Dakota	50	41,670	6,838	48,508
Ohio	223	84,959	19,682	104,641
Oklahoma	85	93,421	16,853	110,274
Oregon	171	47,166	23,307	70,473
Pennsylvania	1,154	535,036	223,464	758,500
Puerto Rico	1	32,027	9,505	41,532
Rhode Island	30	60,691	36,471	97,162
South Carolina	78	166,626	51,776	218,402
South Dakota	43	11,831	5,382	17,213
Tennessee	127	23,571	9,144	32,715
Texas	350	1,001,951	142,301	1,144,252
Utah	74	3,967	645	4,612
Vermont	58	3,574	3,266	6,840
Virginia	206	151,832	53,688	205,520
Washington	152	41,769	9,099	50,868
West Virginia	135	16,119	8,810	24,929
Wisconsin	294	35,692	7,284	42,976
Wyoming	20	3,107	781	3,888
Countrywide	8,382	$10,359,681	$2,102,585	$12,462,266

Sources: National Flood Insurers Association, Insurance Information Institute

Administrator of the United States Department of Housing and Urban Development. Only areas which give assurance that they will enact appropriate zoning regulations and building codes to minimize disastrous floods become eligible for this coverage.

If your property is exposed to the threat of damage by flood, rising surface waters, or similar occurrences, you should take steps to procure flood insurance to the limits available, for this is a hazard which is of a catastrophic nature. An insurance company has been certified as servicing office in each state where this insurance is available and will accept business from any broker or agent.

Insuring against demolition

In some communities, local ordinances prohibit construction of new structures with certain types of material. The regulations sometimes also provide that when a portion of an existing structure of this kind is destroyed, it may not be repaired or rebuilt, and the entire structure must be demolished. In the event such property is damaged by fire or other insured perils, the regular policy will pay only for the actual damage caused. No compensation is made for the portion of the building that must be demolished to comply with the zoning law or ordinance.

A special demolition clause provides insurance against this contingency. This clause is attached to the fire insurance policy. If your present residence faces possible demolition under such ordinances in your locality, you need the addition of demolition insurance to your policy.

Demolition insurance will indemnify only for the actual value of the portion of the building that must be demolished due to ordinance. Thus, if you occupy a frame dwelling in a zone where no further frame construction is permitted, your fire insurance policy will pay only for the actual loss or damage to the property, and the demolition clause will cover the portion of the structure that must be demolished. You cannot collect for the increased cost of reconstructing or repairing in a manner approved by the authorities. Such "increased cost" insurance also may be added in many regions in addition to the regular demolition coverage.

Major Earthquakes in the United States

Year	Locality	Damage
1886	Charleston, S.C.	$ 23,000,000
1898	Mare Island, Calif.	1,400,000
1906	San Francisco, Calif.	24,000,000
	Fire Loss	350,000,000
1925	Santa Barbara, Calif.	8,000,000
1933	Long Beach, Calif.	40,000,000
1935	Helena, Mont.	4,000,000
1940	Imperial Valley, Calif.	6,000,000
1941	Torrance-Gardena, Calif.	1,000,000
1944	Cornwall, Canada-Massena, N.Y.	2,000,000
1946	Hawaii (tsunami damage from earthquake in Aleutians)	25,000,000
1949	Puget Sound, Wash.	25,000,000
1949	Terminal Island, Calif. (oil wells only)	9,000,000
1951	Terminal Island, Calif. (oil wells only)	3,000,000
1952	Kern County, Calif.	60,000,000
1954	Eureka-Arcata, Calif.	2,100,000
1954	Wilkes-Barre, Pa.	1,000,000
1955	Terminal Island, Calif. (oil wells only)	3,000,000
1955	Oakland-Walnut Creek, Calif.	1,000,000
1957	Hawaii (tsunami damage from earthquake in Aleutians)	3,000,000
1957	San Francisco, Calif.	1,000,000
1959	Hebgen Lake, Mont. (damage to timber and roads)	11,000,000
1960	Hawaii and west coast of United States (tsunami damage from earthquake off the coast of Chile)	25,500,000
1961	Terminal Island, Calif. (oil wells only)	4,500,000
1964	Alaska and west coast of United States (tsunami damage from earthquake near Anchorage, Alaska)	500,000,000
1965	Puget Sound, Wash.	12,500,000
1969	Santa Rosa, Calif.	6,000,000
1971	San Fernando, Calif.	553,000,000
1972	Oxnard, Calif.	1,000,000
1973	Hilo, Hawaii	5,600,000

Every state is vulnerable to and has felt the effect of earthquakes. Although insurance against earthquake damage is generally available, relatively few property owners purchase this protection.

Sources: National Geophysical and Solar-Terrestrial Data Center, Insurance Information Institute

Outdoor property insurance

Some fire insurance policies include "walks, yard fixtures, and arbors," but virtually all exclude trees, plants, and shrubbery. The Dwelling Building Broad Form and the Special Form incorporate limited coverage on this class of property, as do the Homeowners package policies. Insurance on yard improvements, trees, landscaping, and other such outdoor property may be attached to fire policies for an additional premium.

Earthquake insurance, mostly in demand on the Pacific Coast but also available elsewhere, may be attached to the fire insurance contract or written in a special policy.

Rental value coverage

All fire insurance policies covering dwellings provide either for an extension of the policy or for an additional amount of insurance to cover the rental value of premises which are rendered untenantable because of fire, lightning, or other perils assumed under the policy. The broad and special forms covering dwellings and the Homeowners package policies afford, as an additional amount, insurance on the rental value of destroyed or damaged premises and the additional living expense incurred after the loss.

The additional living expense coverage of the policy will indemnify an insured person for all necessary living expenses above his usual costs when the extra expense results from a loss covered by the policy. This sum is payable in addition to the amount of indemnity for the actual damages.

Whether you occupy your dwelling property or rent it to others, its use represents rental income and its destruction would deprive you of this income. In view of the high rentals being charged in many sections of the country, it is advisable that you check whether the amount of rental value insurance provided by your policy is sufficient. If it is not, you can purchase additional rental insurance to make up the deficiency.

Similarly, you might estimate the additional living expense which you would incur if you were forced to move out of your damaged or destroyed home, and make sure that the amount of coverage on this risk is adequate in the basic policy.

CHAPTER 15

Protecting
Yourself
Against
Liability
Claims

Each of us is expected to exercise reasonable care to avoid causing injury to our fellows or damage to their property. If, as a result of your negligence, such injury is caused to others, you may be held liable for monetary damages. The degree of care you are called on to exercise differs with each situation, and the question of negligence may be submitted to a jury for a decision.

In addition to the potential liability arising from your participation in sports, business, or other activities, you may face suits for injuries sustained by persons on your premises. The amount of the damages for which you may be held responsible bears little relationship to the value of your property. It is entirely possible, for example, that although your home is worth only $50,000, the courts may decide that damages incurred by persons on the property total $80,000.

Large awards against a homeowner for damages sustained
on his premises may necessitate the loss of the entire property. In more serious cases, even the sale of the property may
not bring enough to meet the court's awards. Because there
is almost no limit on the size of the judgment that may be
entered against a homeowner for damages sustained on his
property, insurance against legal liability of this kind has
been aptly called insurance against possible bankruptcy and
ruin.

Concept of negligence

Owners of property are usually held liable for damages
only when they have been guilty of negligence. A defective
condition on the premises, faulty or improper construction
or repair, or inadequate operation of property—any of these
may lead to a verdict of negligence.

Negligence may be attributed to a homeowner for sins of
either omission or commission. Broadly, if he has done something which a reasonable person would not do under the circumstances, or if he has failed to take precautions which a
reasonable person would ordinarily take under similar conditions, he may be judged guilty of negligence and held liable
for damages.

No exact interpretation can be given for "what a reasonable person would do or would not do under the circumstances." The practical application of the concept of negligence will usually depend on the individual case.

Accidents to persons who enter your premises are not an
everyday occurrence. Nor should it be thought that every injury of this kind will be declared your liability by the courts.
As a matter of fact, such accident claims in which homeowners are found negligent and liable for large amounts of
damages are relatively rare. But there is no question that the
ownership and maintenance of a home involve the risk of
serious liability claims and that the amounts awarded by the
courts may be very high.

Rural homes offer less chance of accidents to passersby
than city dwellings. But all property owners may be held
liable for injuries to guests and to persons such as messen-
gers and inspectors. Even trespassers may recover for dam-

ages under certain conditions. Furthermore, the courts usually recognize a third group of persons who are neither trespassers nor strictly invited guests, but rather "licensees" who visit the property for various reasons.

Care in the maintenance of your premises will no doubt lessen the possibility of damages being assessed against you, but even the most scrupulous homeowner cannot completely eliminate the hazard of legal liability. No one can guarantee that a jury will not decide that a particular accident might have been prevented by reasonable warning or precautionary measures and that the owner is therefore liable for the damages sustained. The jury might also feel that the injuries were caused by a structural defect in the building or premises. Moreover, the property owner may be held liable not only for acts of negligence on his own part but for those of his family, his servants, and others who act as his agents.

Heavy defense costs

Added to the actual damages for which you may be held liable as a property owner would be the possible expenses of defending yourself against legal actions. An action brought against you might be groundless or even fraudulent, but it could cost you a large amount of money to clear yourself. You would be compelled to incur considerable expense in investigating the accident and the circumstances surrounding it, procuring witnesses, and paying court costs, bonds and appeal bonds, and connected expenditures. Such costs can make a serious inroad into your reserves and can exert a heavy drain on your time and energies during protracted periods of litigation.

Comprehensive personal liability

Coverage against the legal liability resulting from your personal actions and the maintenance of your residence is available under a *comprehensive personal liability* policy. The policy is available to any individual, whether he is a homeowner or not, and tenants in rented premises are well advised to provide themselves with this protection. This coverage is also packaged with the property coverages under all Homeowners policies.

The policy covers two distinct sets of hazards. First is the legal liability to persons who enter the premises and suffer bodily injury, sickness, or death. Second is the liability of all the insured persons arising from their nonbusiness activities. The policy will pay all sums for which an insured person is held liable to injured parties—medical expenses, pain and suffering, loss of services, and so forth.

It should be understood, however, that the policy pays only for liability legally imposed on you, except for a stipulated amount of coverage on medical expenses incurred by a person who suffers an accident while on your premises. Like all liability policies, it will not reimburse you for obligations you assume voluntarily or for damages you feel morally bound to pay where no legal liability exists, except for limited medical expenses. Medical payments coverage of $500 is provided under the basic policy and this provision may be increased by the payment of an additional premium. There is no coverage, however, for the medical expenses of anyone insured under the policy.

In a comprehensive personal liability policy, one amount covers all claims by all persons for bodily injury or property damage. Policies may be written for $10,000, $25,000, $50,000, $100,000, or more. The extra charge for increased limits is reasonable and you should endeavor to buy a policy with substantial limits (at least $100,000).

All members of the policyholder's family residing with him, as well as any other person under twenty-one who is in his custody, are insured under the policy. The policy will pay all amounts for which any such person may be held liable for his nonbusiness activities. There is coverage for such liability even when it arises from occurrences away from the insured premises. It would therefore, as an example, apply to suits resulting from sports activities which are brought against the insured person or members of his family who reside with him. There are exclusions under the policy, the chief one relating to the use of automobiles (and watercraft over a certain size), and it should be understood that the comprehensive personal liability coverage, whether written as an individual contract or as part of a Homeowners policy, is not a substitute for automobile liability insurance.

Insurance as a Factor
In Homeownership

The cost of insurance has been a relatively minor factor in the increasing cost of owning and maintaining a home. This table compares the rates of increase in the costs of nine typical homeownership items.

| | Percentage Change | |
	1967-1975	1974-1975
Property insurance	31.4%	5.8%
Property taxes	58.8	5.0
Reshingling a roof	118.7	11.6
Re-siding a house	87.9	9.9
Repairing a furnace	92.3	9.3
Maintenance & repair items	87.6	9.3
Fuel oil & coal	135.3	9.6
Gas & electricity	69.6	16.3
Water & sewer services	69.9	9.8

Sources: Bureau of Labor Statistics, Insurance Information Institute

How Rates Vary for
Comprehensive Personal Liability Policy

This is a typical range of annual rates in effect April, 1976, for $25,000 worth of comprehensive personal liability coverage.

Phoenix, Ariz. $18

Boston, Mass. 14

Birmingham, Ala. 11

Little Rock, Ark. 11

Sources: Insurance Services Office, Insurance Information Institute

The insurance company will defend any suit brought against an insured person that may come within the scope of the policy. The company will also pay most of the premiums on bonds to release attachments, and premiums on appeal bonds, as well as all costs of investigating the accident. If the court taxes the insured with any legal or court expenses, these costs will be borne by the insurance company. It will also be responsible for any interest accruing after a judgment has been entered. In addition, it will pay all expenses for immediate medical and surgical aid necessary at the time of an accident.

All these expenses are payable by the company as additional insurance above the limits of the policy. Under a contract with a limit of $25,000, the company might be called on to pay the full amount of the policy, $25,000, for injuries suffered by one or more persons on the premises, plus court expenses, bonds, the costs of immediate medical aid, and so forth. The policy places no limit on the amount of these extra charges that will be paid except in special instances.

Thus, if a policy provides for a limit of $25,000 for accidental injury to one person and the court awards $30,000 to a claimant, the company will pay $25,000 and any interest or bond charges on this sum only. The insured person will have to pay any interest or other charges on the sum above $25,000 as well as the excess damages. All regular court expenses of the insured person or those taxed against him, however, must be borne by the insurance company regardless of the size of the damages awarded.

Domestic employees' injuries

The liability policy covers accidents caused by a residence employee in the course of his or her work. If an employee is injured while at work and alleges that the injuries were due to the employer's negligence, the policy will defend such a suit and pay any awards, exactly as if the claim were made by an outsider. There is one important exception to this last rule. Where a residence employee is required by state law to be covered for Workmen's Compensation insurance, the comprehensive personal liability policy will not cover, regardless of whether or not the employer has complied with the law and

How Purchases of Liability Insurance Have Increased
(Excluding Auto)

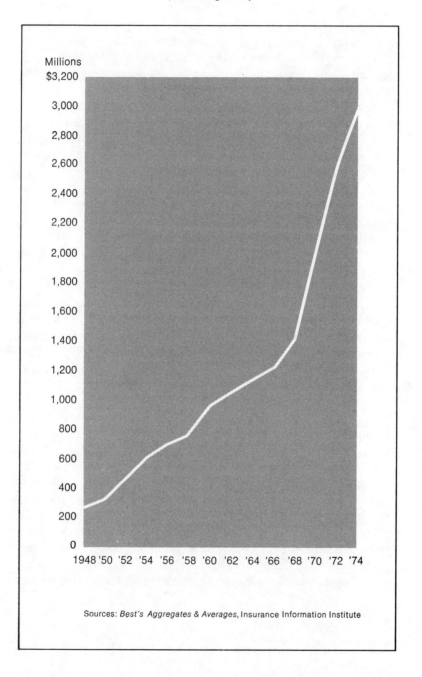

Sources: *Best's Aggregates & Averages,* Insurance Information Institute

obtained a Workmen's Compensation policy. Similarly, when a domestic's employer is not required to carry Workmen's Compensation insurance but elects to do so, the liability policy will not cover a suit brought by the domestic against the employer.

The liability policy insures not only against injuries to persons for which the property owner is legally liable but also against claims arising out of damage to the property of others. Thus, if a tree you are felling damages your neighbor's property or wrecks an automobile, the damage falls within the comprehensive personal liability coverage. The policy will cover the claim for the value of the damaged property and also for the loss of its use to the owner.

Although the comprehensive personal liability policy specifically excludes bodily injury or property damage arising out of the ownership, maintenance, operation, use, loading, or unloading of any motor vehicle or aircraft, it does cover liability arising out of the operation of a boat which does not exceed a stated size or power rating. If the boat is powered by an inboard motor of fifty horsepower or less, the policy will afford coverage, as it will for a sailboat which is under twenty-six feet in length. A boat powered by outboard motor(s) of more than twenty-five total horsepower is not covered under the policy.

If you rent your home and yourself occupy no part of the premises, the tenant is ordinarily responsible for most damages that may ensue. But the transfer of obligation is not complete and you may be held liable for structural or other defects in the property. Even if the lease has been written to relieve you of liability imposed by law on the tenant, you may find yourself jointly responsible for injuries sustained on the premises, particularly if safety ordinances have been violated.

If you should rent your home, especially for a temporary period, do not discontinue your liability insurance, but notify your insurance company of the change in the status of the insured premises.

CHAPTER 16

Insuring Your Household Against Fire

All too often a householder will carry fire insurance for years only to discover at the time of a loss that his policy does not fulfill the purpose for which he has maintained it. Let us then set down the basic rules to follow if you would avoid having inadequate coverage while keeping your insurance outlay down to the absolute minimum.

It is fairly obvious that the first step in insuring your household against fire is to appraise the value of your property. To arrive at such a figure, you need to make an inventory—furniture, appliances, clothing, books, musical instruments, and all other household and personal property. Include in this inventory not only your own property but everything under your roof that belongs to other members of your household, servants, and guests.

It would be best to itemize your property in detail. An

inventory of this kind will serve as a check on articles you might not otherwise be able to recall should fire destroy your home. Futhermore, it can be used to establish not only your need for fire insurance but also for theft, fur, jewelry, and other coverages.

To help in drawing up an inventory of this kind, many insurance companies make available without cost an inventory booklet or property analysis chart. Your insurance agent can usually supply you with such a booklet or chart.

It may be advisable to make some analysis of your property at this time even if you have been carrying fire insurance at a set figure for many years. Often the amount of insurance is either too low or too high because it was arrived at on the basis of a guess. Also, one is often unaware of substantial changes that have taken place quite subtly in the makeup of a family's goods with the passage of time. And today, in view of the marked increases in the cost of most items, a fresh appraisal of your property's current value may be particularly worthwhile.

Figuring value of property

Fire insurance covers your property to the extent of the "actual cash value" but "not exceeding the amount which it would cost to repair or replace the property." You will be making adequate provision if you figure the cost of replacing your property in its present condition. This computation takes into account the present price of an article, which is often higher than when you purchased it, less the depreciation that has taken place through use.

This yardstick of values should be used in estimating the worth of the entire household property. When you have arrived at a figure for the total present value of your property, you are in a position to set the amount of fire insurance you require.

Except in New York State, fire insurance policies for household property are free of restrictions on the amount of insurance that must be carried. In other words, you could cover the full value of the property or buy a policy for less than the full value. In either case, you would collect on any fire loss at your premises up to the amount of the policy. Thus, if your household goods are worth $10,000 and you have a policy for $5,000, the company will pay up to $5,000 for damage inflicted on your property by fire. In such a case, if your loss is greater than $5,000, you would have to bear the loss above $5,000 yourself.

Insure for full value

Even though you may be free to set your own insurance figure, it is recommended that the fire insurance be equal to the full amount of your household value. This is especially true with regard to a smaller home, the chances of total or near-total loss being greater in the case of a smaller household than in a more elaborate one. And in fire insurance, as in all forms of insurance, it is precisely the heavy loss, less likely though it is, that we are least equipped to bear and that needs to be shifted to an insuring company.

Furthermore, even if the amount of insurance you are carrying is equal to the full value of your property, it is likely that through the natural tendency to add to your household and the impact of inflation, the value of your property will soon outstrip your insurance.

For the more elaborate household, as in the case of the smaller one, a great deal can be said for full-value insurance. There is always the risk of a total loss even on a larger residence. This hazard is increased, of course, in districts which are not within easy reach of regularly manned fire-fighting equipment.

The more extensive household in protected areas—those within easy reach of regularly staffed fire-fighting stations —can be protected adequately with insurance of 80 percent of the total value of the property covered. With rare exceptions, setting the insurance figure at less than 80 percent is a risky practice that may force an insured person to absorb a heavy loss.

Coinsurance requirements

Policies issued on property in New York State usually contain a coinsurance clause, which makes it essential to cover at least 80 percent of household values. If you carry less than 80 percent insurance, you will receive only a portion of any loss you suffer. In such cases, the company's liability is limited to that proportion of any loss you suffer that the amount of insurance bears to 80 percent of the value of your property at the time of the loss.

To illustrate this point, let us say that your household property in New York is worth $50,000 and you are carrying $25,000 of fire insurance. You feel quite confident that any fire that might break out will be brought under control before it has caused more than $25,000 damage to your home. When fire does strike, it damages property worth only $4,000 and you sit back securely with your $25,000 of insurance to cover this $4,000 loss. Then you discover that your policy's provisions regarding coinsurance clearly limit the company's liability, in this instance to 62.5 percent of any loss you suffer— the proportion that $25,000 (amount of insurance) bears to 80 percent of the actual cash value of the property, in this case $40,000 (80 percent of $50,000). This proportion is expressed as follows:

$$\frac{\$25,000 \text{ (amount of insurance)}}{\left.\begin{array}{l}\$40,000 \text{ (80 percent of actual} \\ \text{value of property}\end{array}\right\}} = \frac{5}{8} \text{ or } 62.5 \text{ percent}$$

This percentage is used by the company in adjusting any loss you suffer regardless of its size. In this instance, you would be entitled to $2,500 of the $4,000 you lost in the fire.

Had you insured properly with $40,000 coverage (80 percent of the $50,000 your property is worth), you would receive 100 percent indemnity for any loss you suffered up to the amount of the policy.

It is important, too, to bear in mind that this coinsurance clause contains the words "at the time such loss should happen." This means that the amount of insurance you should carry must comply with the 80 percent provision at the time the loss occurs, not at the time you took out the policy. It is consequently no defense to show that the insurance was large enough when you bought the policy in relation to the value of the household at that time. All additions to your household property since the policy was issued, as well as augmented values arising from increases in the cost of goods, will be taken into account at the time of the loss to determine

Leading Causes of Fire in Buildings

Causes of Ignition	Number of Fires in 1974 Sub-Total	Total	Percent
Trash Burning		177,000	15.9
Electrical		165,000	14.8
Wiring distribution equipment	112,200		
Motors and appliances	52,800		
Heating and Cooking Equipment		160,000	14.4
Defective or misused equipment	93,300		
Chimneys and flues	14,000		
Hot ashes and coals	12,600		
Combustibles near heaters and stoves	40,100		
Smoking-Related		121,600	10.9
Incendiary and Suspicious		114,400	10.3
Open Flames and Sparks		77,500	7.0
Sparks and embers	13,300		
Welding and cutting	11,600		
Friction, sparks from machinery	11,900		
Thawing pipes	5,800		
Other open flames	34,900		
Children and Fire		59,600	5.4
Flammable Liquids		56,100	5.0
Exposure		44,200	4.0
Lightning		16,600	1.5
Gas Fires and Explosions		11,900	1.1
Spontaneous Ignition		11,000	1.0
Fireworks and Explosives		4,200	.4
Miscellaneous Known Causes		91,700	8.3
Unknown Causes		159,200	
Totals		1,270,000	100.0

Sources: National Fire Protection Association estimates, Insurance Information Institute

whether you are meeting the requirements of the coinsurance clause.

Underinsured and overinsured

The history of losses during recent years indicates that many households which were adequately protected when the policies were written are not today carrying sufficient insurance to offset current increased prices.

Conversely, being overinsured is a waste of money and should be avoided. It is advisable to have a fire policy large enough to cover likely additions to your furnishings or wardrobe so that you do not have to increase your insurance every time you buy an item of value, but there is no point in carrying insurance that covers more than the actual worth of your property.

Replacing your policy

If you are buying household fire insurance for the first time or are starting from scratch with a new policy, you will be able to utilize the recommendations in Chapter 13 to insure properly at the lowest cost to yourself. In event you are covered under a household fire policy taken out some time ago, it may have been written at an unfavorable rate. Should you drop your present policy and buy a new one? Unfortunately, this cannot be recommended without qualification.

The company will cancel your present policy (it is your privilege to cancel at any time), but it will compute the earned portion of the premium according to a special table, the short-rate table. Under this table, the company is allowed to retain a larger part of the premium than has been earned on a proportionate basis, retaining 20 percent of the premium for one elapsed month, 30 percent for two months, and so forth. This extra charge upon cancellation will generally offset most of the savings possible in a company using more favorable rates, so it will be just as well if you wait until the policy comes up for renewal before replacing it.

You might attach a note to the policy now to remind you that its renewal requires attention. Or you could notify your broker or agent now regarding the policy that is to replace the current one.

It is important to understand that fire insurance policies are subject to a minimum premium, regardless of the amount of coverage. Thus, assume there is a rate of 39 cents per $100 of insurance for an apartment in a brick building in a large city. A $5,000 policy would incur an annual charge of $19.50 but the policy would be written for $25, the minimum premium in most areas.

CHAPTER 17

Insuring
Your
Household
Against Theft

While insurance against fire loss to households is fairly wide-spread today, protection against the hazard of theft is often lacking.

Many householders are put off by what they believe to be the costs of theft insurance. They also sometimes forgo this insurance because of an incorrect understanding of the coverage it provides.

Whether you are at present insured under a Homeowners package policy or a theft policy or are seeking this protection for the first time, you should know how to achieve the maximum of protection at the lowest possible cost. Substantial reductions in the cost of theft insurance are often possible not only in the case of the larger household, but even more commonly in the smaller household with a minimum of valuables.

The Broad Form Personal Theft policy has been widened

considerably since it was first introduced. It now is not merely a burglary policy to cover losses when your premises are broken into but also covers virtually every act of stealing. This includes larceny, which is almost any unlawful taking of property, and robbery—any loss where violence or the threat of violence is used to induce you to part with your property, as in a holdup. Mysterious disappearance, except of a precious or semiprecious stone from its setting, is also covered, as is all damage to premises and insured property during theft or attempted theft or by vandalism or malicious mischief.

The protection against larceny, burglary, robbery, and mysterious disappearance provided in the policy can be extended to cover all your insured property while anywhere in the world. The "theft away from the premises" clause, like the coverage on the premises, covers your own property and that of all permanent members of your household, usually including residence employees. The policy agrees to pay for actual loss of such property and for damage to such property and the premises caused by theft or attempted theft.

The loss of your wife's luggage on a train or at a resort; a holdup perpetrated on your son on his way home from a theater; your daughter suddenly missing her watch in a restaurant; your pocket picked; the laundry stolen from the basement—all these are examples of losses that can come within the scope of the Broad Form Personal Theft policy.

How to determine coverage needed

As in the buying of fire insurance, the first requisite for a theft insurance program is to determine the amount of coverage required. As a basis for arriving at this figure, you can refer to the inventory of household values you drew up for your fire insurance. In this instance, however, you need figure only the property more likely to be stolen or damaged. The best dollar values in theft insurance will be realized by dividing the property to be insured into the following three groups:

Group 1. The more valuable items of property that are subject to the peril of theft. Describe each item in this group separately and state its value. Items in Group 1 might be:

    1 man's Bulova watch, 14-kt. gold case $150
    1 diamond engagement ring $600
    1 set Gorham sterling silver, service for 8 $750

Group 2. Jewelry items only. For this group, figure the combined value of all jewelry items which you did not list in Group 1. It is not necessary in this second group to describe or value the items separately. Simply set one amount in dollars to cover the aggregate value of this jewelry. In addition to such items as necklaces, bracelets, earrings, brooches, and rings, consider as jewelry all these types of property: watches, precious and semiprecious stones, and articles of gold, platinum, and sterling silver.

Since you will have listed the more expensive items in Group 1, Group 2 will include the smaller jewelry items, for which you will state a single value, e.g., $500.

Group 3. "All other property" to be insured against theft which has not been covered in Groups 1 and 2. In totaling the value of the property in this group, you should begin by taking into account the easily portable items. This should include clothing, linens, rugs, clocks, ornaments, lamps, tableware (except if sterling silver), kitchen equipment, luggage, television sets, radios, typewriters, sewing machines, golf clubs, cameras, sports equipment, and the like.

You should omit all fur articles from the theft policy if you decide to obtain comprehensive coverage on furs in a special policy, as is recommended in Chapter 18.

When you have made a survey and decided on how much insurance you require on all items that warrant protection against theft, add about 20 percent to provide some latitude and to cover damage to doors, windows, and furniture by burglars. This 20 percent figure to be added to your policy is only an estimate. You may deem it too high or too low for your particular needs. The important thing to bear in mind is that some additional coverage should be provided for damage to property and premises. Damage of this kind has been known to reach considerable proportions, as when burglars break cabinets, vases, and the like in their search for hidden valuables.

You can now arrive at a figure for Group 3, which will consist of property which might be stolen, other than jewelry

Crimes Against Property

(000 omitted)

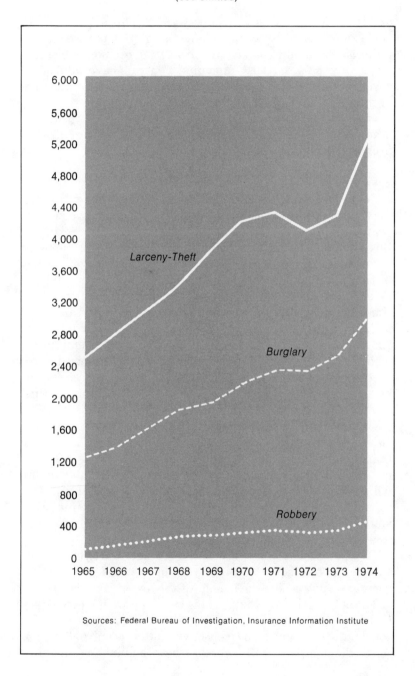

Sources: Federal Bureau of Investigation, Insurance Information Institute

and items insured under Groups 1 and 2, plus an addition of some 20 percent, plus cash on hand up to $100, plus securities up to $500. Should you require protection on money or securities in excess of these amounts, you can have additional coverage on these items written into your policy for an extra premium.

If the valuable "theft away from the premises" insurance is added to a Broad Form Personal Theft policy, an additional premium must be paid for it.

Saving on premiums

Try to have your Broad Form Personal Theft policy written for three years to save 30 percent of the premium every three years. In the event you find it difficult to meet the larger three-year premium, you do not have to pay the full amount in advance. You may pay the premium on a three-year policy in three annual installments, but in this event you will not receive any discount; the three-year premium will be three times the annual. You may find it advisable to do this if the policy you are buying would not require a premium of at least $25 on a one-year basis, as $25 is the minimum premium for which a Broad Form Personal Theft policy will be issued. Also, buying a three-year policy, even if you do not receive the benefit of a reduction in premium, will protect you against any increase in rate during the term of the policy.

Underwriting considerations frequently result in a narrower selection of Broad Form Personal Theft insurance than of fire insurance on household property. As a consequence, you may be limited in your efforts to find a company which offers savings on this type of insurance. The effort should be made, however, and some assurance obtained that you are not paying more than is necessary for this form of coverage.

If your present policy is written for one year, you may be able to have it rewritten now for three years in the same company and receive the benefit of the lower rate charged.

To replace a policy you are now carrying with a new policy from another company, it is better to wait until the policy comes up for renewal. If you have your present policy canceled, the company will compute the premium for any time

Increased Spending for Theft Insurance
(1948-1974)

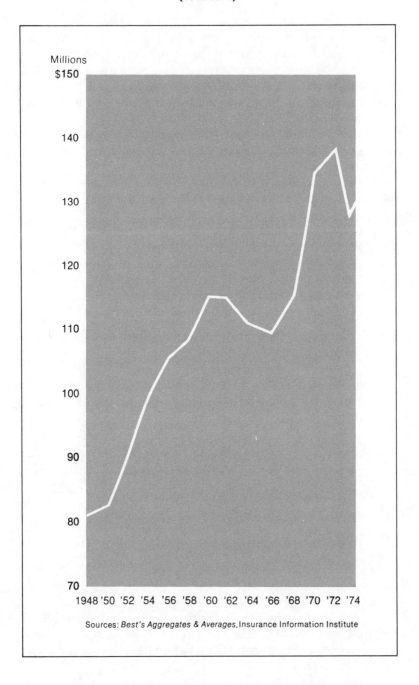

Millions
$150

140

130

120

110

100

90

80

70

1948 '50 '52 '54 '56 '58 '60 '62 '64 '66 '68 '70 '72 '74

Sources: *Best's Aggregates & Averages,* Insurance Information Institute

elapsed according to the short-rate table. The portion of the premium retained by the company for the elapsed time will be larger than the proportionate time involved, and this extra charge may wipe out any savings you anticipate under the new policy.

If you are at present carrying a theft policy which you plan to replace with one from another company at expiration, attach a reminder to the policy about its replacement or notify your agent or broker now of your wishes in the matter of its renewal.

To illustrate how you can save on theft insurance, let us assume a household contains the following:

1 lady's diamond ring	$600
Man's watch, semiprecious earrings, clips, gold wedding band, cuff links, sterling silver cigarette lighter, and all other jewelry items belonging to the family	$400
"All other property," which includes clothing, linens, pictures, draperies, rugs, clocks, ornaments, lamps, tableware (not sterling), kitchen equipment, luggage, TV sets, radios, typewriters, sewing machine, golf clubs, cameras, fishing equipment, and the like	$1,500
20 percent additional to provide some latitude and to cover damage to premises and property during theft or attempted theft	$300
Cash on hand and usually carried by household members (limited to $100 unless increased by payment of additional premium)	$100
Securities on hand	$100

It is fairly common to find insurance on such a household written without breaking the property down according to type. Even though the total of all values listed above is $3,000, a policy of $2,000 might be written under the "blanket" form, which provides that the protection apply to any and all property regardless of type.

Assuming the premises you are insuring to be an apartment in Los Angeles, a $2,000 policy on the 100 percent blanket form will cost $78.63 for a year, including $1,000 of "theft away from the premises" insurance.

Let us see what results are achieved when we follow the previously described recommendations for buying theft insurance.

First, we fit the policy to the specific makeup of the property. We insure the $600 diamond ring specifically, cover the smaller miscellaneous jewelry items with $400 of insurance, and the balance of property with $1,500 of insurance—a total of $2,500. The diamond ring is insured for both on and off the premises, and we add an additional $1,000 for "theft away from the premises," which is quite adequate for this particular situation. This policy, covering the household fully, carries an annual premium of $59.66, as compared with $78.63 for the 100 percent blanket policy, a reduction of over 24 percent in cost.

In addition, if the policy were written for a period of three years, the net outlay for the three years might be reduced to $161.08. This would be an average of $53.69 a year instead of $78.63, a reduction of over 31 percent, without any additional economies that might be realized from a more competitive company.

Even if your household and personal property are of a more modest nature, you can effect considerable economies in your theft insurance outlay.

Let us assume you do without sterling silver tableware, expensive rings, and watches. The total value of all jewelry, consisting of a few semiprecious items, is $100. A household situation such as this is frequently covered by $1,000 of 100 percent blanket insurance. In our same Los Angeles apartment, this policy costs $49.40 for one year, with $1,000 of "theft away from the premises" insurance.

By adapting the policy to the property values, your premium outlay is reduced to $33.50, and might be further reduced to an average annual outlay of $30.15 when written for three years, for a combined saving of just under 39 percent.

Your requirements for coverage against theft may be best met by obtaining one of the Homeowners package policies and these should be checked out as well as separate theft insurance when comparing costs.

CHAPTER 18

Special Insurance for Personal Articles

The Personal Articles Floater provides all-risk insurance on furs, jewelry, cameras, silverware, musical instruments, golfers' equipment, stamp and coin collections, and fine arts.

It should be emphasized that the Broad Form Personal Theft policy, even when written to cover furs or jewelry, does not apply to any articles of this kind which are specifically insured in another policy, such as the Personal Articles Floater. Therefore, full value should be placed on items being insured under the floater.

Insuring furs

This floater may include any article of fur—coats, hats, scarves, muffs—as well as any article in which fur represents the principal value, as in a fur-trimmed cloth coat. Each item to be insured must be specified in the policy with its value.

When you apply for this insurance, you will be asked for some proof of the value you ascribe to each article. A bill of sale or an appraisal from a furrier is usually considered sufficient evidence of the actual value of a fur item. Most companies will also accept the values stated in a previous fur policy.

While the floater calls for specifically scheduling each fur article to be covered, there is some insurance for a limited period on newly acquired property. Such property is covered for an amount not exceeding 25 percent of the insurance in force on scheduled items, but for no more than $10,000 in any event.

To be covered on such nonscheduled items, the insured person is required to report their acquisition within thirty days and to pay the additional premium arising from the increase in coverage.

The floater for furs differs from fire and theft policies in that it provides "all-risk" coverage. Protection is afforded against loss or damage in all situations with the exception of perils specifically listed in the policy. The risks excluded are:

• wear and tear, gradual deterioration, insects, vermin, or inherent vice

• a series of perils related to actions of war

• any weapon of war employing atomic fission or radioactive force, whether in peace or war

• a series of perils related to insurrection, revolution, and similar occurrences

• contraband or illegal transportation or trade

• a series of perils related to nuclear reaction

Risks which would not be covered by fire and theft policies but are clearly within the range of the floater include loss or damage from windstorm, earthquake, explosion, or water. Also, the often expensive repairs to accidentally torn furs would be collectible under the floater, as would damage from paints, acids, or chemicals.

Costs vary widely

Insuring furs for $1,000 under a floater costs over four times as much in Los Angeles County as it does in Connecticut, Indiana, Iowa, Michigan, Minnesota, North Carolina, North Dakota, Ohio, South Dakota, or Wisconsin.

It is necessary to make a comparison of costs in each individual situation, particularly if large values are involved. Unless there is a sizable saving to be realized by covering the fur items in the separate fire and theft policies, the Personal Articles Floater might be considered because of its all-risk nature.

There is usually little difference in cost compared with the combined premiums for fire and theft insurance covering the same furs. If anything, the floater will be cheaper in most areas than insuring this same property in fire and theft policies. This more comprehensive coverage is therefore often recommended on all furs.

The discount that was formerly offered on three-year fur floaters has been withdrawn in most of the states. Three-year policies are now written at 2.7 times the annual rate only in Hawaii, Kentucky, Mississippi, Pennsylvania, and Rhode Island.

In Texas, the three-year rate is 2.78; in Puerto Rico, it is 2.5 times the annual rate.

Where a discount for the three-year policy is available, you should of course take advantage of it.

Insuring jewelry

Articles of jewelry are generally regarded among the most hazardous of the property values in the average household. Though items of furniture or apparel may actually cost more, the nature of jewelry makes it subject to greater risks of loss.

Because of the high degree of hazard inherent in these valuables, many owners feel it important to protect their jewelry with all-risk insurance under a Personal Articles Floater. While there is no doubt that this special policy on jewelry offers the most comprehensive insurance possible, widening of the coverage in other policy forms can provide adequate jewelry protection at a lower cost than is charged for the floater.

Because of a decrease in demand for insurance on jewelry, particularly for larger articles, you may find little choice when trying to obtain such coverage. If your jewelry is valued at a fairly high figure, you might ask to compare the cost of insuring under a Personal Articles Floater with the premiums for separate fire (and allied perils) and theft policies.

The floater covering jewelry agrees to pay for all risks of loss or damage, with a few exceptions listed in the policy. The excluded hazards are the same as those applicable to furs with some variations for the specific nature of the property. Thus, a stipulation is added to cover loss of articles which are part of a pair or set. In such situations, the policy states that the measure of loss shall be a fair proportion of the total value of the pair or set, giving consideration to the importance of the article or articles without however considering the loss a total one.

Superior coverage on jewels

This form of insurance is obviously superior to separate fire and theft policies, not only in the extra hazards that are clearly assumed by the floater—windstorm, explosion, earthquake, and the more common hazards of chipping and breaking—but in the very way the insurance is written. The question of the company's liability is somewhat less likely to arise under a floater.

There is another type of situation in which loss of jewelry might not be covered fully except by a floater. Such a loss would involve destruction of jewelry by fire when away from the insured premises. The regular household fire policy will, as a matter of course, cover fire loss on jewelry which occurs at the premises. But at most, only 10 percent of the amount of the fire policy applies to loss by fire on property when temporarily removed to another location. Furthermore, the coverage for loss occurring away from the premises is restricted to the United States and Canada, so damage to your jewelry by fire when you are traveling outside of these two countries would not be covered at all under the fire insurance policy.

Despite these deficiencies, fire and theft policies can be counted on to cover the large majority of jewelry losses. A Broad Form Personal Theft policy would generally cover losses of this kind, except if a precious or semiprecious stone disappears from its setting. Although such losses are not assumed under the theft policy, they would be covered under a

Personal Articles Floater, as would less usual losses or damage, such as cracking or chipping.

There can be no question that the coverage of the Personal Articles Floater is broader than that available under separate policies covering against specific perils. Unless the cost of insuring your jewelry under the floater is substantially higher than other insurance on this property, you should provide yourself with the more inclusive insurance. Again, as in the case of furs, rates vary widely in different areas, although the spread is not as extreme as it is for furs. An area that has a very high rate for jewelry under the floater may not be rated as high for theft. In New York City, for example, the rate for theft insurance in Kings County is about 20 percent higher than in Queens. The rate for the jewelry floater in both counties is identical.

The situation in respect to savings on three-year policies for jewelry is the same as for furs.

Insuring photographic equipment

If you own expensive cameras, projectors, or other photographic equipment, you may be interested in the Personal Articles Floater's all-risk insurance. A comparison between the two methods of insuring this type of property will help you decide, in light of the additional costs involved, whether your situation calls for this wider protection.

In the floater, you may include photographic property of any kind—cameras, projectors, and accessories, as well as materials and equipment used in developing, printing, enlarging, retouching, and so forth. It is also permissible to include binoculars, telescopes, microscopes, and other items used in conjunction with photography.

Each article to be insured must be scheduled in the policy with its value, as in the case of furs or jewelry, but with this exception: when insuring photographic equipment under a floater, you may apply up to 10 percent of the amount of the policy to cover miscellaneous materials. Thus, if your floater lists and describes specific cameras and equipment totaling $500, you may add up to $50 to cover miscellaneous items. This unscheduled property may include any photographic materials except films, which must be listed specifically in the schedule of the floater. As in the policy's coverage on furs, the floater also grants automatic insurance on newly acquired photographic property for a period of thirty days.

Choices for amateur photographers

If you do not work at photography commercially, you can give consideration to insuring your cameras and photographic equipment under your regular residence policies or the floater. The floater premium for cameras and related equipment is nationwide, except for Texas, which has rates up to 20 percent higher than the rest of the country, and North Carolina, where rates are slightly lower than in other states. By contrast, the rates for fire insurance and particularly the Broad Form Personal Theft policy range widely throughout the country. To determine what savings, if any, may be realized by insuring under your regular residence policies will require an analysis of costs under both approaches.

Any economies you may be in a position to secure must be seen in the light of the differences in coverage. The fairly extensive coverage of the theft policy comprises the hazards of burglary, larceny, robbery, vandalism, malicious mischief, and mysterious disappearance, and these perils can be covered not only at your premises but worldwide. Your photographic property, if you are in the amateur class, can be included with your other household items in a Broad Form Personal Theft policy.

The household fire policy would also cover this equipment, without special provision, as part of your regular property. Any loss or damage by fire occurring at the insured premises would be covered by the policy, with 10 percent of the amount of insurance applying to fire losses on property temporarily removed to another location within the United States or Canada. Under these two policies, then, your camera and photographic materials can receive fairly adequate insurance against the perils of fire and theft, the latter understood, of course, in the broad sense that the policy provides.

Because of the special hazards of breakage, as well as water damage, windstorm, explosion, smoke, and such perils which threaten your cameras and allied materials, you may prefer the broader coverage of the floater. When you insure under a floater, you provide all-risk insurance, and you can therefore omit this property from your fire and theft policies. This will result in some saving on the cost of these two policies.

Insuring musical instruments

Another type of property which may be insured under a Personal Articles Floater is musical instruments. As in the case of cameras, the policy requires scheduling all items to be covered except that miscellaneous musical property such as strings, reeds, tuning forks, and sheet music may be insured on a blanket basis for an amount not exceeding 10 percent of the value of all scheduled property.

Separate rates apply for professional and nonprofessional use of instruments. Rates for professional musicians vary and can be as much as six times higher than for amateurs.

It is extremely important that you be clear on the use of the word "professional" in the policy. A floater with the nonprofessional rate schedule contains a representation by the insured which states that "none of the instruments hereunder will be played for remuneration during the term of this policy unless otherwise endorsed hereon and additional premium paid at the current rates of the company." Note that the restriction would apply to the playing of an instrument for payment even if by an insured person who is not a professional musician in the usual sense of the word. It would appear to apply even to lending an insured instrument to a nonprofessional who might be playing for pay at a local dance or church affair.

Insuring works of art

The Personal Articles Floater may be written to cover the fine arts. This class of property includes paintings, etchings, tapestries, and other bona fide works of art (such as valuable rugs, statuary, antique furniture, rare books, antique silver, manuscripts, porcelains, rare glass, and bric-a-brac) of rarity, historical value, or artistic merit.

Coverage and conditions for property of this nature are similar to those discussed in connection with the other classes of property insurable under a Personal Articles Floater. However, risks located in Florida and certain areas in Alabama, Mississippi, Louisiana, and Texas call for special endorsement and the payment of an additional premium to cover the perils of windstorm, tornado, and hurricane.

There is also a special exclusion in the fine arts schedule of a floater which must be understood. The policy does not cover breakage of statuary, glassware, bric-a-brac, porcelains, and similar fragile articles unless caused by fire, lightning, aircraft, theft and/or attempted theft, cyclone, tornado, windstorm, earthquake, flood, explosion, malicious damage, or collision, derailment or overturn of conveyances. The ordinary breakage of property of this kind due to accidental dropping of the object is not covered by the policy but can be included by paying an additional premium.

Personal Effects Floater for travelers

The personal effects you carry with you when traveling are subject to increased hazards of loss or damage against which you may feel it important to provide. Insurance on such property is often purchased in a Personal Effects Floater.

The extra outlay for this floater is not warranted in most instances, since little or no addition to the regular residence policies need be made to cover an ordinary trip or vacation. But there are special circumstances which call for the extra protection of the Personal Effects Floater.

When you apply for this type of floater, you will not be asked to submit a list of the articles you wish to insure, as you are required to do under the Personal Articles Floater. Instead, your policy will be read "on all personal effects as are usually carried by tourists and travelers belonging to or used by or worn by the insured and/or his wife and their unmarried children residing together."

Excluded from insurance under this floater are the following types of property:

- household furniture
- animals
- accounts, bills, currency, deeds, evidences of debt, letters of credit, passports, documents, notes, securities
- automobiles, motors, motorcycles, bicycles, boats, or other conveyances or their appurtenances, automobile robes

- salesman's samples, merchandise held for sale or exhibition, theatrical property of any kind
- railroad and other tickets
- physicians' and surgeons' instruments
- artificial teeth or limbs
- any property specifically or otherwise insured

The Personal Effects Floater differs from the other floaters discussed in that it covers the insured property only when away from the premises. Since your personal effects are generally taken off your premises for temporary periods only, you will have to provide for these articles when on the premises in your regular fire and theft policies. You cannot therefore consider this floater complete insurance on personal effects but rather an addition to the residence policies. It is from this point of view that you should analyze the floater to determine what extra protection it affords.

Limitations in floater

The Personal Effects Floater, like all floaters, provides coverage against all risks of loss or damage except those specifically listed in the contract. This floater, however, in addition to the usual exclusions, contains several limitations which narrow its scope. The policy does not cover property on the premises of the insured or stored in a public warehouse. It does not cover theft from unattended automobiles unless there is evidence of forcible entry. Even when such marks of force have been left by the burglar, the company's liability is limited to 10 percent of the amount of insurance and to not more than $250 for all property in any one loss. This restriction can be removed from the policy upon payment of an additional premium.

While the floater covers the insured and/or his wife and their unmarried children, it will not indemnify for any loss suffered by students while in fraternity or sorority houses, dormitories, or on the premises of schools and colleges, except when the loss is caused by fire. This exclusion can be eliminated too, but again only by paying an additional premium.

Coverage on breakage of articles of a brittle nature, one of the more important advantages of most floaters, is limited in the Personal Effects Floater to breakage caused by thieves, fire, or accident to conveyances.

Floater compared with other policies

These special limitations of the Personal Effects Floater must be kept in mind in any comparison of this insurance with fire and theft policies. Remember that the scope of the theft policy's coverage is fairly broad and that worldwide protection is afforded under its "theft away from the premises" section. Included in the policy are the hazards of burglary, robbery, larceny, vandalism, malicious mischief, and mysterious disappearance. Insurance is granted not only against loss but also against damage to property arising from these perils. Thus, breakage caused by thieves is covered under the terms of the policy. The theft policy then, when properly written, is fairly comprehensive in scope and covers the great majority of property perils.

Moreover, in considering the Personal Effects Floater, you will find the rather unusual situation where hazards which are excluded from the floater are covered by the theft policy. Thus, if you were to suffer a loss by theft from an unattended automobile, the theft policy would pay but the floater would not. If your car is broken into and marks of force are left by the burglar, the theft policy, unlike the floater, does not impose a percentage limitation on the insurance company's liability.

Also, any loss or damage insured by the theft policy will be paid in full up to the amount of insurance, regardless of the nature of the property. The floater will pay only up to 10 percent of the amount of the policy on jewelry, watches, or furs, with not more than $100 on any one such article.

Students' property in schools, colleges, dormitories, and fraternity or sorority houses is covered under the theft policy, as is property on the premises of the policyholder and stored in public warehouses. In these respects at least, the Broad Form Theft Policy is more comprehensive than the all-risk Personal Effects Floater.

Advantages of floater

Advantages of the floater include its coverage of losses

arising from windstorm, earthquake, explosion, water damage, smoke and smudge, acids and other harmful chemicals, and any other peril not specifically excluded by the policy.

Some superiority in fire protection may also be afforded by the floater, which covers items fully against fire, with the exception of the limits on jewelry, watches, and furs already outlined. Without a Personal Effects Floater, a property loss by fire when away from the premises is covered by most household fire policies, but only up to 10 percent of the insurance carried, and then only when the property is within the United States or Canada. Subject to this 10 percent limit, breakage due to fire is also covered under the household fire policy. One type of breakage is covered only by the Personal Effects Floater—breakage due to an accident to a conveyance.

Against these advantages of the floater must be balanced the fact that coverage against fire and theft will usually have been provided which encompasses the majority of risks to which your personal effects may be exposed. The cost of the floater will therefore be in addition to this regular insurance.

The premium for a Personal Effects Floater is generally computed at 1 percent of the amount of insurance plus a flat charge of $15. Thus, a $1,000 floater of this kind will carry an annual premium of $25. A floater with a $25 deductible is available at $7.50 plus 1 percent of the policy amount.

If the floater is dropped before a full year has elapsed, as is fairly common, part of the premium will be returned. But the amount retained by the company for the elapsed time will be reckoned according to the short-rate table. While there is no set minimum, it is a common practice to charge $15 as a minimum premium, regardless of how long the floater was kept in force.

You may find that your personal effects do not require any addition to your basic fire and theft policies if these contracts have been drawn up correctly. The only exception to this rule might be an increase in the amount of "theft away from the premises" insurance in your theft policy if the value of the personal effects you plan to take on your travels is unusually high.

If you have given up your home completely to take an extended trip and have no permanent address, you will not be in a position to provide insurance on your personal effects in household fire and theft policies. This applies, too, to transients living in hotels who have no permanent address. If your furniture is in storage, you can cover this property with fire and theft policies, but your theft policy will not contain the important "theft away from the premises" insurance, without which your personal effects will not be covered. In such situations, the Personal Effects Floater may fill a need in your insurance picture.

Traveling salesmen and professional actors and entertainers should pay special attention to the exclusions listed earlier in this chapter and note that samples, merchandise held for sale, and theatrical property cannot be insured under this floater.

If you are in one of the groups requiring a special policy on personal effects, or insist on adding the extra protections of this floater to the regular policies covering your home, you will have difficulty in finding companies with competitive rates because of the somewhat limited demand for this coverage. There is no reason, of course, why you should not seek the best rates available, but do not expect too much in the way of economies when buying this form of protection.

CHAPTER 19

Package
Policies

With policies covering your residence, its contents, the risk of theft, and personal liability, you will have fairly complete insurance against the hazards of owning property. However, more and more homeowners and tenants are purchasing special policies which combine these coverages into a single contract.

In most states, there are five "package" policies, of which four are offered to owners of private residences and one to tenants in rented premises. The four homeowners' forms are made available in most states only to owner-occupants of private homes, although some twenty states also permit the use of these forms to owner-occupants of two-, three-, and four-family dwellings.

Each of these forms is made up of a basic policy jacket which sets forth on the first page the general insuring agree-

Rising Popularity of
Homeowner "Package" Policies
(1958-1974)

Until the mid-1950s, few homeowners carried adequate insurance to protect against financial losses resulting from predictable perils. The insurance
industry then successfully developed homeowner "package" policies offering
coverage against a variety of perils. This chart shows the increasing expenditures for such policies.

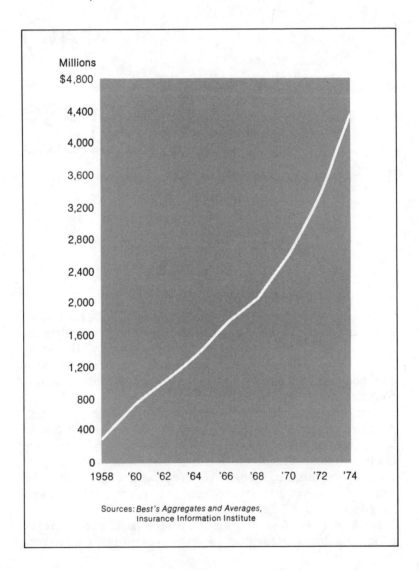

Sources: *Best's Aggregates and Averages,*
Insurance Information Institute

Example of Homeowners Policy—Broad Form

	Amount of Coverage	
Property Coverages	*Insured to Value*	*Insured at 80%*
Dwelling	$25,000 *(full value)*	$20,000 *(80% of full value)*
Appurtenant private structures	2,500 *(10% of dwelling)*	2,000 *(10% of dwelling)*
Unscheduled personal property	12,500 *(50% of dwelling)*	10,000 *(50% of dwelling)*
Additional living expenses	5,000 *(20% of dwelling)*	4,000 *(20% of dwelling)*
Liability Coverages		
Personal liability	$25,000 (each occurrence)*	$25,000 (each occurrence)*
Medical payments to others	500 (each person)*	500 (each person)*
Physical damage to property of others	250 (each occurrence)	250 (each occurrence)

*Larger amounts are available.
Source: Insurance Information Institute

ments, the declarations of the insured person, and certain information about the risk for rating purposes. The second page embodies the provisions of the standard fire insurance policy, while the third and fourth pages state the general conditions and definitions of the policy. To this basic jacket is attached one of the four homeowner forms—1, 2, 3, or 5.

Form 4 is issued to persons who rent homes or tenants of apartment houses. It provides the coverage of the broad form policy on the contents and the comprehensive personal liability policy, together with additional living expenses.

Each of the forms for homeowners (1, 2, 3, and 5) covers

the dwelling, its contents, and additional living expenses. Theft is also covered. Liability insurance which is virtually identical with the comprehensive personal liability policy is included in a separate section of the policy.

The minimum amount of coverage on the dwelling under these policies is $8,000, except for Form 5, which has a minimum of $15,000. All of these policies cover related outbuildings (garages, tool sheds, guest houses, and so forth) for 10 percent of the amount of insurance on the main dwelling. Coverage of $5,000 is provided for second homes located within the same state as the principal residence.

Personal property—the contents of the premises—is covered for 50 percent of the amount of insurance on the house. This figure may be reduced to 40 percent in all policies except Form 5. The amount of insurance on the contents may be increased under any of the four forms. On personal property away from the premises, each policy provides coverage up to 10 percent of the amount of insurance on this property while it is in the house with a minimum of $1,000, except that under Form 5 the coverage off the premises is the same as on the premises—50 percent of the dwelling limit.

Forms 1 and 2 extend the policy to cover up to 10 percent of the dwelling amount on additional living expenses, while Forms 3 and 5 grant 20 percent for this coverage. All cover trees, shrubs, and plants, and may also be endorsed with scheduled articles on an all-risk basis at the same rates as under the Personal Articles Floater described in Chapter 18.

The most important differences among these four policies are in the perils covered, with Form 1 the most restricted on this score and Form 5 the most comprehensive.

Form 1 provides protection against the perils covered by the fire insurance policy (fire and lightning), the extended coverage endorsement (windstorm, hail, explosion, riot, riot attending a strike, civil commotion, aircraft, vehicles, and smoke), theft, glass breakage, and vandalism and malicious mischief. This policy has the lowest premium cost of all the Homeowners forms.

Form 2 provides broader coverage than Form 1 and adds to the narrower contract the perils covered by the broad form dwelling policy discussed in Chapter 14.

Example of Cost of
Insuring $25,000 House

Coverage	Insured to Value		Insured at 80%	
	Cost Per Year	Cost Per Month	Cost Per Year	Cost Per Month
Basic Form—11 perils*	$111	$ 9.25	$ 88	$ 7.33
Broad Form—18 perils*	$126	$10.50	$ 99	$ 8.25
Comprehensive Form —"all risks"*	$182	$15.17	$144	$12.00

*$100 deductible.
Source: Insurance Information Institute

How Homeowner Policy Rates Vary

This is a typical range of annual rates for insuring a $25,000 frame house in April, 1976, under Homeowners Form 3, the most popular of the package policies. Companies' rates vary for the coverage.

(With $100 deductible)
Boston, Mass. $208

Phoenix, Ariz. 152

Birmingham, Ala. 143

(With $50 deductible)
Little Rock, Ark. 146

Sources: Insurance Services Office, Insurance Information Institute

Form 3 provides the same coverage on contents as Form 2, i.e., the perils in the fire policy, the extended coverage endorsement, and the Dwelling Building and Contents Broad Form. It differs from Form 2 in that it affords all-risk insurance on the dwelling akin to the Dwelling Building Special Form.

Form 5 provides the most comprehensive protection available in the insurance industry on the dwelling and the contents, both of which are insured on an all-risk basis. Its premium naturally is the highest of all the Homeowners forms.

In deciding on the form to buy, your chief considerations will be the premium cost and your attitude towards insuring yourself against perils of various kinds. Unless your home is furnished in an elaborate and expensive fashion, you can probably forgo the coverage of Form 5. Adequate coverage for most homeowners is afforded under Form 3 with its all-risk insurance on the dwelling and impressive list of perils on the contents. If the premium charges for this form are too onerous, you can cut back to Form 2 and, finally, to the most limited, Form 1.

The package policies, as we have seen, are structured with set amounts of insurance on contents, based on the value of the dwelling. Some homeowners may find that the amount of insurance on contents in these policies is more than they require. Others may feel that they do not need to carry theft insurance on the contents. In such cases, a cost comparison should be made of other policies covering the dwelling and the amount of coverage on contents. The study should take into account the cost of providing adequate limits under a comprehensive personal liability policy and insuring the dwelling for at least 80 percent of the replacement cost.

Generally, it will be found that the cost of the package policy will be close to what separate fire insurance on the dwelling and contents and a comprehensive personal liability policy would cost without theft insurance. Packaging is therefore a way to obtain some theft insurance at little cost.

PART FIVE
Automobile Insurance

CHAPTER 20

Protection
Against
Automobile
Liability
Claims

Most automobile owners recognize the need to provide some insurance against injuries or damages that may be caused by their vehicles. The importance of adequate protection of this kind is emphasized by special laws in most states which restrict the right of persons to drive or own a motor vehicle after they have been involved in an accident, unless they are carrying insurance or can establish their financial responsibility in some alternate method acceptable in their state.

The cost of fully insuring an automobile, however, is usually quite high, and many car owners are forced to forgo some important aspects of this protection or to content themselves with less than adequate coverage.

It is important that you understand your individual need for the different forms of automobile insurance, the broad outlines of the statutes in your state covering the right to

drive and own a car, and how to make the most economical use
of your insurance premium dollars.

If you own an automobile, you are faced with two groups
of hazards. First, there is the threat of damage or complete
loss of the automobile itself; second, the damage that your car
may cause to persons or property.

Of these two types of hazard, the first is the less serious because although your car may be one of the most expensive
property items you own, even its total destruction cannot exceed the value of the automobile. By contrast, the total cost of
claims to which you may be subjected because of accidents is
almost unlimited. Injury to persons and damage to property
may easily total many times the worth of your automobile,
and judgments entered against you might wipe out not only
your car but also other property you own. In addition, to
satisfy a court's judgment against you because of an automobile accident, your actual earnings may be attached within
limits set by law.

Relatively very few car owners possess sufficient cash or
liquid assets to meet large claims for injury or death which
may be assessed against them. Almost all car owners will
have to depend on insurance to protect themselves against
such claims.

In addition to the damages for which you might be held
liable, defending yourself against lawsuits could cost you a
large sum of money. Investigating the accident and all the
circumstances surrounding it, procuring witnesses, court expenses, bonds, and appeal bonds could add up to a sizable
figure even if the case is ultimately decided in your favor.

Liability for injury or death

An automobile liability insurance policy will pay for the
liability that is imposed on you by law to persons who suffer
bodily injury or death. Under this feature, the insurance company pays any sums awarded by the courts for the medical
care and expenses of the injured person, for his loss of time
and services during recovery, and for his pain and suffering.
(The relatively recent no-fault statutes enacted in some states
put limitations on the compensation for "pain and suffering.")

Economic Losses From Traffic Accidents

Increases in traffic accidents, injuries, and deaths, coupled with the rising costs of automobile repairs and medical care, in recent years have pushed the total dollar cost of highway crashes to a new peak. In the last 50 years, nearly 2 million persons have died in some 616 million traffic accidents in the United States, with the overall cost estimated at $387 billion. The economic loss figure includes the cost of paying for property damage and legal, medical, hospital, and funeral bills, as well as loss of income and the administrative costs of insurance.

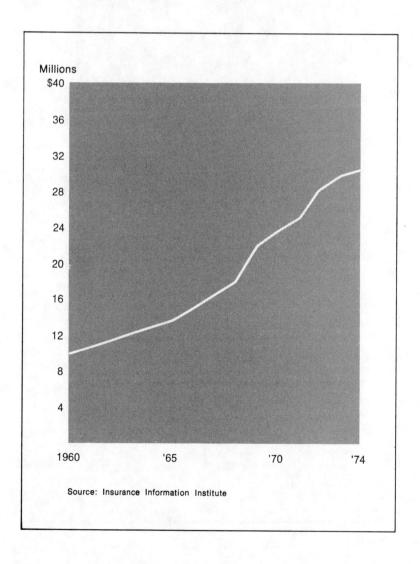

Source: Insurance Information Institute

Motor Vehicle Deaths

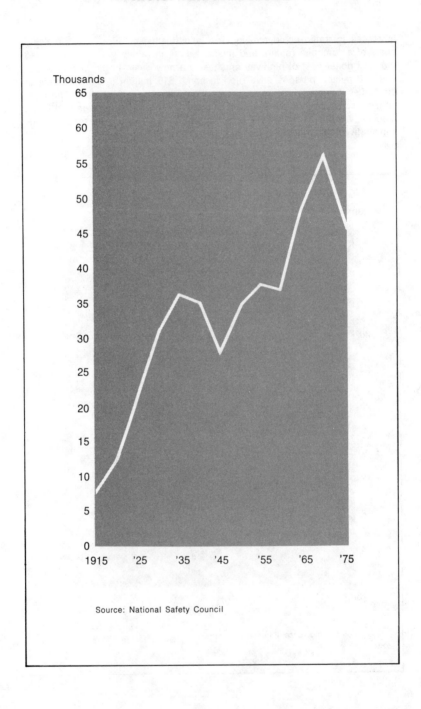

Thousands

Source: National Safety Council

It should be understood, however, that the policy pays only for liability imposed on you. It will not reimburse you for obligations you assume voluntarily or for damages you feel morally obligated to pay where no legal liability exists. Further, the policy does not cover injuries you sustain personally, except to some extent under the optional medical payments coverage in your policy and within the limits now in operation in no-fault states.

Automobile liability policies are generally written with three limits, e.g., $10,000, $20,000, and $5,000. The first figure is the maximum that the insurance company will pay for all claims arising out of injuries to one person. *Subject to this limit per person,* the policy will pay up to $20,000 (the second limit) for all claims arising because of injuries to more than one person in a single accident. The third limit, $5,000, is the maximum payable under the policy for damage to the property of others for which the insured person is held liable.

By way of example, assume a person insured under an automobile liability policy with limits of $10,000, $20,000, and $5,000 (or 10/20/5, as it is known) becomes involved in an accident which injures three individuals. A is awarded $3,500 by the court; B is awarded $12,000; and C, $5,000. The policy will pay $3,500 to A, $10,000 to B, and $5,000 to C. Note that B receives from the insurance company only $10,000 of the $12,000 awarded him by the court even though the $20,000 second limit of the policy has not been exhausted.

Question of negligence

Traditionally, proof of negligence has been the key to recovery of monetary damages by a person injured in an accident for which a motorist was responsible. The motorist's negligence might have been purely negative, as when he failed to do something that "a reasonable person would ordinarily have done under normal circumstances." If he had done something that a "reasonable person would not have done under similar circumstances," he might also be declared negligent.

By the end of 1975, twenty-five states and Puerto Rico had enacted automobile insurance reform legislation, including no-fault laws, providing for direct payments of out-of-pocket

Automobile Insurance Reforms

The following jurisdictions have adopted auto insurance reforms effective on the dates shown:

Compulsory First-Party and Liability Insurance;
Some Restrictions on Lawsuits

Colorado, April 1, 1974	Michigan, October 1, 1973
Connecticut, January 1, 1973	Minnesota, January 1, 1975
Florida, January 1, 1972	Nevada, February 1, 1974
Georgia, March 1, 1975	New Jersey, January 1, 1973
Hawaii, September 1, 1974	New York, February 1, 1974
Kansas, January 1, 1974	North Dakota, January 1, 1976
Kentucky, July 1, 1975	Pennsylvania, July 19, 1975
Massachusetts, January 1, 1971	Utah, January 1, 1974

Puerto Rico, 1970

Compulsory First-Party and Liability Insurance;
No Restrictions on Lawsuits

Delaware, January 1, 1972	Maryland, January 1, 1973

South Carolina, October 1, 1974

Insurance Not Compulsory; First-Party Benefits Optional;
No Restrictions on Lawsuits

Arkansas, July 1, 1974	Texas, August 27, 1973
*Oregon, January 1, 1972	Virginia, January 1, 1972
South Dakota, January 1, 1972	Wisconsin, May 18, 1972

*First-party coverages must be provided in liability insurance policies covering private passenger vehicles.

Source: Insurance Information Institute

losses to injured persons by their own insurance companies.

Specific restrictions on lawsuits (or negligence action) are included in the laws of Colorado, Connecticut, Florida, Georgia, Hawaii, Kansas, Kentucky, Massachusetts, Michigan, Minnesota, Nevada, New Jersey, New York, North Dakota, Pennsylvania, Utah, and Puerto Rico.

While the laws of the other nine states discourage lawsuits by mandating or requiring the offer of "first-party" injury insurance—payable without regard to fault—they include no bars to legal action. Those states are: Arkansas, Delaware, Maryland, Oregon, South Carolina, South Dakota, Texas, Virginia, and Wisconsin.

In the rest of the country, the concept of negligence is still fully applicable, although there is no rule that can be applied to ascertain negligence. There are instances, it is true, where a driver's negligence is quite clear, as when he violates traffic ordinances or operates a vehicle under conditions which render him incapable of exercising normal restraint or judgment. Thus, driving when intoxicated would generally be sufficient to establish negligence in an accident, as would passing a stop light or failing to heed other warning signals.

Usually, the question is more involved, as when defective tires or faulty brakes are cited as the possible cause of an accident. Even in the relatively clear-cut cases, there is always some question possible. Did the driver violate a given traffic law? Was he actually incapable of exercising normal judgment? Were these conditions the direct cause of the accident? There may also be questions regarding the conduct of the injured person and his part in the accident.

The question of a driver's negligence in a particular accident will usually be a matter for decision by the courts. During recent years, an increasing number of traffic accident cases is being decided by juries, who generally have considerable latitude in finding whether negligence was involved.

"Contributory negligence"

In many states, when the injured person has not exercised reasonable care, he is guilty of "contributory negligence" and the owner of the car is not held liable for the accident. The precise nature of contributory negligence permits wide interpretation but even if the claimant placed himself in a fairly obvious position of danger by his actions, the operator of the automobile may, in some jurisdictions, still be declared liable if it can be shown that he had a "last clear chance" to avoid injuring the other person and failed to exercise it.

There are further ramifications of this question which apply in special cases. Thus, some courts have ruled that no child under seven years of age is capable of contributory negligence. A youngster between the ages of seven and fourteen may also be declared incapable of contributory negligence unless he can be shown to possess the intelligence and judgment of an average child of fourteen.

In Alaska, California, Florida, Mississippi, New York, Rhode Island, Washington, and Puerto Rico, a plaintiff's rights will not be lost by his contributory negligence but only reduced in proportion to his contribution to the accident.

In Connecticut, Massachusetts, Montana, Nevada, New Hampshire, New Jersey, Oregon, South Carolina, Texas, Vermont, and Wisconsin, a plaintiff may recover where his negligence was not greater than the defendant's.

In Arkansas, Colorado, Georgia, Hawaii, Idaho, Kansas, Maine, Minnesota, North Dakota, Oklahoma, Utah, and Wyoming, a plaintiff may recover where his negligence was not as great as the defendant's.

In Nebraska and South Dakota, the contributory negligence of the plaintiff does not bar him from winning damages if his negligence was slight when compared with the negligence of the defendant.

All in all, it is apparent that the most careful driver may find himself liable for inflicting accidental injuries, even on persons who have not been diligent in avoiding injury.

Vicarious liability

While it is true that as a general rule the owner of a motor vehicle is not liable for accidents by other persons using his automobile, vicarious liability statutes have been enacted in thirty-nine states, the District of Columbia, and Puerto Rico. The scope of these laws varies widely, ranging from those which impose liability on the owner for any accidents caused by the driver's negligence (California, Connecticut, Idaho,

Iowa, Massachusetts, Michigan, Minnesota, New York, North Carolina, Rhode Island, Tennessee, the District of Columbia, and Puerto Rico) to those which hold the owner liable for accidents caused by minors who operate the vehicle while unlicensed (Arizona and Virginia).

A number of states (Alaska, Arizona, Arkansas, California, Colorado, Delaware, Florida, Hawaii, Idaho, Indiana, Kentucky, Maryland, Mississippi, Montana, Nevada, New Mexico, North Dakota, Ohio, Oklahoma, Rhode Island, South Carolina, Tennessee, Texas, Utah, and Wisconsin), Puerto Rico, and the Virgin Islands require the parent or guardian of a minor to sign his application for an operator's license and make the signer jointly and separately liable for damages caused by the minor.

It is important to understand that such liability is imposed on the parent or guardian for accidents involving any car driven by the minor, whether the car is owned by the parent or not. Such liability can be imposed even when a parent or guardian is not a resident of a state which has this statute in effect if the accident occurs in such a state.

Liability for others who may drive his car imposes an additional responsibility on the owner of a motor vehicle. He must provide for possible claims of this kind as well as for the results of his own actions.

State laws outlined

While compulsory automobile liability statutes are in effect in only twenty-two states, Puerto Rico, and the Virgin Islands, all the states have enacted legislation which limits the right to own or operate a motor vehicle after its owner or operator has been involved in an accident. Such laws are also in effect in Canada.

The scope of these laws varies in the states but their provisions tend to fall into two major groups. First, virtually all the financial responsibility laws, also known as guaranteed safety or safety responsibility laws, demand that drivers convicted of certain offenses establish their financial responsibility or provide insurance. Until they furnish such proof, their right to operate an automobile is suspended. Most of these states also revoke or severely limit the registration license of

State Financial Responsibility Laws

In most states, a minimum amount of property damage must be involved before the requirements of the financial responsibility laws are invoked. Below are the minimums established under the statutes of the various states:

$50 Minimum
Alabama

$100 Minimum
Colorado
District of Columbia
Georgia
Hawaii
Idaho
Mississippi
Missouri
Oklahoma
Vermont
West Virginia

$150 Minimum
Ohio

$200 Minimum
Alaska
Florida
Indiana
Kentucky
Louisiana
Maine
New Jersey
New York
North Carolina
North Dakota
Oregon
Pennsylvania
Rhode Island
Tennessee
Utah
Washington
Wisconsin

$250 Minimum
Arkansas
California
Delaware
Illinois
Iowa
Nebraska
Nevada
Texas
Virginia
Wyoming

$300 Minimum
Arizona
New Hampshire

$400 Minimum
Connecticut

Source: Insurance Information Institute

the automobile involved. Furthermore, the majority of these laws apply to motorists convicted of designated offenses even outside their home state or in Canada.

The offenses which most commonly lead to suspension where no insurance is carried are reckless driving, failing to stop after an accident, driving while intoxicated or under the influence of narcotics, and a record of convictions. All states except Maryland and Massachusetts require that proof of financial responsibility of stipulated minimum amounts be filed after certain convictions.

In twenty-two jurisdictions the law requires that any person involved in an accident post security sufficient to satisfy the expected judgment. Such security requirements can be met by showing that the person had an automobile liability policy of not less than the prescribed limits in effect at the time of the accident, or by posting a bond, or by depositing cash or securities in the amount set forth in the statute, or by proving self-insurance. Such laws are in effect in Alabama, Arizona, Delaware, Florida, Georgia, Hawaii, Idaho, Iowa, Louisiana, Maryland, Mississippi, Nevada, New Jersey, New York, Ohio, Oklahoma, Pennsylvania, Rhode Island, Tennessee, Washington, Wyoming, and the District of Columbia.

In sixteen other states, the posting of security is required of any driver deemed to have been at fault in an accident. Those states are Alaska, Arkansas, Colorado, Connecticut, Illinois, Maine, Missouri, Nebraska, New Hampshire, North Carolina, North Dakota, Texas, Utah, Vermont, West Virginia, and Wisconsin.

Twenty states require proof of financial responsibility to satisfy the possible judgment after an accident and also proof of financial responsibility for any future accidents. Such proof for future accidents is usually required only when the driver's fault can be proved. The period of time during which such proof must be maintained varies by state. Such statutes are in effect in Alaska, Arizona, Arkansas, California, Colorado, Florida, Georgia, Indiana, Louisiana, Maine, Mississippi, Nebraska, New Hampshire, Oklahoma, Oregon, Tennessee, Texas, Vermont, Virginia, and Washington.

While there are some differences among the states in the application of their financial responsibility laws, they all re-

Automobile Liability Insurance Requirements

In many states the minimum limits of automobile liability insurance to satisfy the requirements of financial responsibility laws are $10,000 for all claims arising out of injuries to one person, $20,000 for all claims in any one accident for injuries to more than one person, and $5,000 for property damage claims. States with other limits are:

5/10/1

Louisiana

5/10/5

Massachusetts

Oklahoma

10/20/2

Missouri

12.5/25/7.5

Ohio

15/30/5

California

Colorado

Florida

Kansas

Nebraska

Nevada

New Jersey

New Mexico

North Carolina

Oregon

Pennsylvania

South Carolina

South Dakota

Utah*

Washington

Wisconsin

15/30/10

Arizona

Indiana

20/40/5

Connecticut

Maryland

New Hampshire

20/40/10

Maine

Michigan

25/50/5

Virginia

25/50/10

Alaska

Minnesota

25/unlimited/10

Hawaii

*May be a single limit of $25,000.

Source: Insurance Information Institute

quire that a person against whom a judgment has been entered satisfy it before his license to operate or register a motor vehicle is restored. A judgment is considered satisfied, regardless of its amount, when a sum equal to the limit in the financial responsibility law has been paid. In most of the states, a person against whom a judgment has been entered must also post proof of financial responsibility to pay for any future accidents.

The majority of the states have established reciprocity to make their financial responsibility laws applicable to accidents which occur in other states as well as within their own borders.

If there was in effect at the time of an accident a valid automobile liability insurance policy equal to or larger than the limits prescribed in the state's financial responsibility law, the licenses of the car owner and the operator will not be suspended, regardless of the amount of the claim or judgment.

Automobile liability insurance may be purchased with broader limits than the usual 10/20/5—25/50/10, 100/300/ 10, 500/1,000/25, as examples. These higher limits are applied in the same way on accidents to individuals and on each accident as the 10/20/5 limits.

What insurance covers

Any amounts for which the insured person may be declared liable by the courts because of his ownership, maintenance, or use of his automobile will be paid by the company subject to the limits in the policy. These sums represent only one of the two types of possible loss accepted by the insurance company under an automobile liability policy. In addition, the company will defend any suits brought against the insured person for accidents that come within the scope of the policy.

The company will also pay most of the premiums on bonds to release attachments, and premiums on appeal bonds, as well as all costs of investigating the accident. If the court taxes the policyholder with legal expenses, these costs will also be borne by the company. It will be responsible too for any interest accruing after a judgment has been entered. Finally, it will pay all the expenses of immediate medical and surgical treatment necessary at the time of the accident.

All of the expenses which have been outlined are payable by the company as additional insurance above the limits of the policy. Under an automobile liability policy with 25/50 limits, then, the company might be called on to pay as much as $25,000 for all claims arising out of injuries to one person, plus court expenses, bonds, immediate first aid, and so forth. The policy places no limit on the amount of these extra charges that will be paid except in certain special instances. Thus, if the policy provides for a limit of $25,000 for claims arising out of injuries to one person, and the court awards him $30,000, the policy will pay $25,000 (its limit) and interest charges on this amount only. The policyholder will have to pay any interest or other charges on the sum above $25,000 as well as the excess damages. All regular court expenses of the insured person or those levied against him must be borne by the insurance company.

The automobile liability policy covers not only the policyholder but also any person using his automobile with permission and any person or organization legally responsible for the use of the vehicle.

It does not cover injuries to the insured person himself, except for stipulated medical expenses, nor to employees other than domestics who may be injured in the course of their employment. Excluded too are accidents arising from the operation of an automobile repair shop, public garage, sales agency, service station, or public parking place.

Drive-other-car coverage

The family automobile policy covers the insured person and his spouse while driving other automobiles which are not furnished for their regular use. Coverage would actually extend to their driving an automobile of the commercial type, provided its use was not in connection with their business. Relatives who reside with the insured person are also covered while driving private passenger automobiles which are not furnished for their regular use.

This drive-other-car coverage applies only when the vehicle is operated with the permission of its owner. If this automobile is withdrawn from normal use because of breakdown, repair, loss, or destruction, and the insured person temporarily uses another automobile not owned by him, the substitute vehicle is covered under the policy.

Rates vary greatly

Rates for liability insurance on automobiles vary sharply. The most important factors affecting the premium for this insurance are the area in which the automobile is principally garaged and the classification of the principal operator. There are three methods of rating and several hundred classifications for drivers.

Generally, automobile insurance is issued on the basis of a signed application from the owner of the vehicle. The application is designed to elicit information about the automobile, its use, its place of principal garaging, the ages of the operators, the accident records of the operators, violations and convictions, and other matters on which the underwriters base their acceptance of the risk and the rate to be charged.

It cannot be stressed too strongly that all questions on the application should be answered accurately and completely. Because automobile liability insurance frequently carries a high premium, automobile owners have resorted to misrepresentation to cut the cost of insurance. Thus, as examples, the automobile is "registered" at a location which is rated lower than the actual place of garaging; the age of the insured—an important factor for male operators under the age of twenty-five—is misstated; or the insured's occupation is incorrectly stated. There is widespread belief that such misrepresentations cannot result in coverage being denied. At worst, it is frequently contended, the company will be able to collect the additional premium that would have been required if the application had been completed correctly.

Actually, there is an impressive array of court decisions which hold such misrepresentations to be grounds for denial of coverage. Over a quarter of a century ago, a court in a western state held that an insurance company could deny liability for an accident which involved an insured person who had improperly represented that his automobile was principally garaged in a community which had a lower premium than the city in which the vehicle was actually garaged.

Numerous cases in which the insured person represented

Rates Decrease
As Young Drivers Grow Older

These charts are based on a driver classification plan in use by a large segment of the insurance business. The rates shown are for drivers in Des Moines, Iowa, where rates are in the medium range. The coverage provided is 10/20/10 liability insurance, $1,000 medical payments, uninsured motorist coverage, $50 deductible comprehensive, and $200 deductible collision. These rates are for youthful drivers with "clean" driving records who operate 1976 full-size private passenger cars for pleasure only. Adjustments in premiums are made for cars used to drive to work, used for business, or used on a farm. Adjustments are also made for youngsters with driver training credit, drivers with "unclean" records, and owners of more than one car. In many states, premium discounts are available to students with outstanding scholastic records.

Unmarried male operator under age 30 who owns or is a principal operator of the automobile

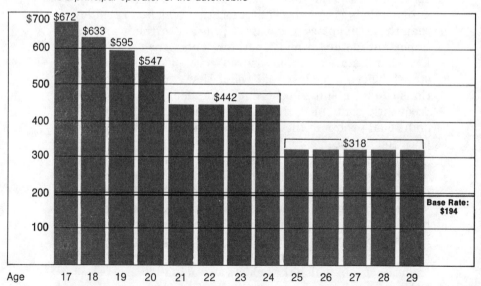

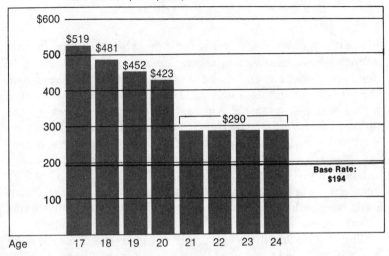

Unmarried male operator under age 25 who is not the owner or principal operator

- $519
- $481
- $452
- $423
- $290
- Base Rate: $194

Age: 17 18 19 20 21 22 23 24

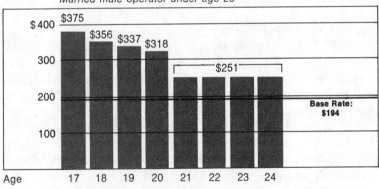

Married male operator under age 25

- $375
- $356
- $337
- $318
- $251
- Base Rate: $194

Age: 17 18 19 20 21 22 23 24

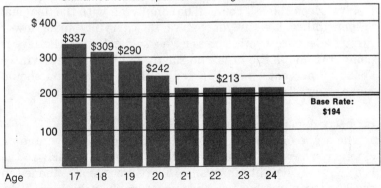

Unmarried female operator under age 25

- $337
- $309
- $290
- $242
- $213
- Base Rate: $194

Age: 17 18 19 20 21 22 23 24

Source: Insurance Information Institute

himself as twenty-five years of age when he was in fact younger have established the insurance company's right to deny coverage. Recently, the Wisconsin Supreme Court held that the policy did not cover an accident in which the insured man's nineteen-year-old son had been involved because the application submitted by the father had stated that there were no drivers under the age of twenty-five resident in his household.

Similarly, incorrect statements about the policyholder's accident record and a failure to disclose previous convictions have been held to void the coverage, as have misstatements about previous cancellations of automobile coverage.

There is no doubt that an applicant is risking financial disaster if he fails to answer all questions truthfully at the time he applies for automobile insurance.

Juries award large sums

In all forms of insurance it is the risk of the large loss which the average individual is least able to carry himself that should be shifted to the insurance company. Automobile claims have long involved large sums and the inflation of recent years has sent them even higher.

In view of these facts it is recommended that your automobile liability insurance be written with not less than 100,000/300,000 limits. A policy of this kind will provide $100,000 of insurance on all claims arising out of injuries to one person and $300,000 on all claims for injuries to more than one person in an accident. Such insurance cannot be considered excessive. Even though you will be complying with the financial responsibility law in your state by carrying much lower limits, adequate protection for yourself calls for the larger policy. Although the premium for these higher limits will be about 40 percent more than for a 10/20 policy, you should make every effort to meet the increased cost.

Property damage coverage

The scope of the automobile liability policy's coverage on claims for damage to the property of others is similar to the bodily injury liability insurance. The coverage is extended in the same way to other persons operating the vehicle with the permission of the insured. The policy covers the actual cost of repairing or replacing the damaged property and also the loss of its use to its owner. Also covered, over and above the limits of the policy, are the expenses of defending suits brought for claims that come under the policy and court costs levied against the insured person in such actions. The insurance does not apply to damage to the insured automobile nor to any property owned by, rented to, in charge of, or transported by the policyholder.

Accidents which cause property damage may result in suspension of driving and registration licenses, even when bodily injuries are not inflicted. In thirty-nine states and the District of Columbia, property damage liability insurance of $5,000 is required to comply with the financial responsibility laws. In Alaska, Arizona, Hawaii, Indiana, Maine, Michigan, Minnesota, and South Dakota, the laws call for not less than $10,000 of coverage against property damage liability. In Louisiana, only $1,000 need be carried, while Missouri requires $2,000 and Ohio's minimum is $7,500.

While $5,000 of property damage liability insurance will serve to comply with the financial responsibility laws of most states, this amount of insurance is inadequate today. An accident causing damage to two cars can easily involve more than $5,000 of damages, and an automobile out of control can plough into a store front and cause damage much in excess of this sum. Your automobile policy should provide at least $10,000 of coverage against these risks. Increasing property damage liability from $5,000 to $10,000 will add about 5 percent to the premium. Remembering that it is the catastrophic occurrence you need to be protected against, this extra outlay can be seen as well warranted.

Guest laws

Except in states which have enacted some form of no-fault legislation, compensation for bodily injury or property damage is not usually granted unless the individual claiming damage can prove negligence on the part of the defendant. The automobile liability policy, in such cases, covers only bodily injuries or property damage for which the owner or driver of the car is deemed legally liable by the courts.

In many states, guests who ride in an automobile are restricted in their right to take legal action against the owner of the vehicle, even when an accident results from the driver's negligence. Under the terms of these special laws, guest occupants of a car may not be able to collect for injuries sustained in the same accident for which an injured pedestrian or occupant of another car would be entitled to collect.

In states with no-fault laws, the effect of the guest laws has been considerably modified. All the state no-fault laws provide for some degree of direct benefits for medical expenses and loss of earnings without reference to fault. Covered persons under these laws include the owner of an automobile, relatives who are members of his household, occupants of the vehicle at the time of the accident, and generally pedestrians who are struck by the insured auto.

Guest laws are in effect in Alabama, Arkansas, California, Delaware, Idaho, Illinois, Indiana, Iowa, Massachusetts, Michigan, Nebraska, Nevada, New Mexico, North Dakota, Ohio, Oregon, South Carolina, South Dakota, Texas, Utah, Virginia, and Wyoming. The provisions of these laws differ among the states, but they all require as a minimum that the driver be guilty of gross negligence before a guest can take legal action to recover for injuries suffered while riding as a passenger in a private automobile.

Some guest laws are even more restrictive and permit a guest to sue only when the driver was intoxicated or guilty of "willful or wanton misconduct" or "reckless disregard of the rights of others."

A guest is usually defined as anyone who has not paid for his transportation although courts have sometimes interpreted the word more liberally in favor of the injured person. In specific cases, some courts have held that when the driver or owner could receive any benefit from the presence of his passenger, such a person is not a guest and may recover if ordinary negligence was the cause of the accident. But generally the guest laws operate to eliminate legal action by most passengers, including members of the car owner's family.

Optional coverage

Many car owners feel an obligation toward those who may

be injured in their vehicle even though they may not be legally liable for their passengers' injuries or are residents of a state in which a guest law is operative. As an option, the automobile liability policy makes available coverage on the medical, surgical, hospital, ambulance, and nursing expenses of those who are injured while riding in, entering, or alighting from the policyholder's car. In the event of accidental death under these circumstances, the funeral expenses will be paid. This coverage is direct reimbursement to the injured person and is completely apart from any question of negligence. It also covers the insured person.

This supplementary protection is usually offered with a maximum limit of $5,000. The limit of insurance under this extra feature is not an aggregate amount but applies to each passenger injured or killed. Under a medical payment provision with a limit of $500, any number of guests injured in the same accident would be entitled to reimbursement from the company for their medical expenses. Each passenger could receive as much as $500.

In states which do not have a guest law, a passenger could bring suit and win damages when the driver was guilty of negligence. In such states, a guest passenger is in much the same position as any pedestrian or other person outside the car. Medical payments coverage in these states offer some indemnity for the medical expenses of guests when negligence on the part of the driver of the car is not involved or when guests do not care to file a suit, as well as for the expenses of members of your own family and for your own injuries when you are included in the special coverage.

In states where a guest law is in effect, this extra feature will provide somewhat wider coverage. In addition to payments in the situations outlined above, it will pay for some of the medical expenses of guests injured in your car who are prevented from filing a suit against you by a guest law.

In all cases, the coverage under this feature is limited to medical expenses incurred by the injured person. No indemnity is paid for the loss of time or services. Since the amount of insurance is quite limited in the medical payments provision, it will not cover the consequences of more serious accidents and cannot therefore be considered an essential of an

Comparative Costs of Coverage

Bodily Injury Liability Insurance

In an area where	10/20	costs	$55 a year
you can buy	25/50	for	$76 a year
and	50/100	for	$90 a year
or	100/300	for	$104 a year

Property Damage Liability Insurance

In an area where	$ 5,000 costs	$32 a year
	$10,000 costs	$34 a year
	$25,000 costs	$35 a year

Medical Payments Insurance

In an area where	$ 500 coverage costs	$ 8 a year
you can buy	$ 1,000 coverage for	$10 a year
and	$ 2,000 coverage for	$12 a year
or	$ 5,000 coverage for	$15 a year
or	$10,000 coverage for	$23 a year

Source: Insurance Information Institute

automobile insurance program. Certainly, this extra feature should not be purchased at the expense of adequate limits on the liability policy itself. If you have to choose between the two, it is sounder to elect the larger liability limits and forgo the medical payments coverage. The threat of a $100,000 suit brought against you by an injured person when you are carrying only $10,000 of liability insurance for such an accident is far more serious than the limited medical payments which the company will pay to you or to passengers who might not be in a position to recover through a lawsuit for their injuries.

Premium rates increase rapidly

Automobile liability insurance is not written for more than one year. Because of the rapid increase in premium rates for this insurance during recent years, some companies are issuing policies for only six months.

Auto insurance premiums increased about 46 percent between 1967 and 1975. However, this was considerably less than the increase in the costs of items for which auto insurance pays. These items include hospital service charges for a semiprivate room, which rose over 136 percent in the 1967-75 period; automobile repairs and maintenance, up nearly 77 percent; physicians' fees, up more than 69 percent; and all medical care items, up more than 68 percent.

In automobile insurance, as in coverage on your other personal property, no particular type of company can be cited as offering the best buys. Competition among insurers is replacing the earlier situation where rates were fairly well standardized.

Stock companies, mutual companies, direct writers, mail-order companies, companies affiliated with motor clubs, department stores, and professional organizations all compete actively for the automobile insurance premium dollar. The soundest course to follow is to do some comparison shopping, provided certain precautions are taken.

First, in the case of automobile insurance as in any other form, you should buy from a company which is admitted to do business in your home state. A call or written inquiry addressed to your state's insurance department can tell you whether a particular company has been admitted to your state and therefore subject to the jurisdiction of your state regulatory officials.

It is also generally advisable to pick a company which is licensed in all states or at least in all those through which you are likely to drive. Finally, remember that cost should not be the only criterion for the selection of a company. The company's reputation in claim handling and the services of a broker or agent who is competent and reliable must also be weighed in the scale of values.

21

Coverage
for
Your Car

While accidental injury and property damage are the most
serious consequences of the ownership, maintenance, or use
of an automobile, the car owner has an additional cause for
concern—his investment in a vehicle which faces the threat
of damage or destruction from several perils. To protect this
investment, you can purchase insurance against the more
common of these hazards.

While coverage is offered against specific perils, such as
fire, lightning, smoke, smudge, and theft, most automobiles
are insured under a policy which includes all risks except
collision. The contract which specifies perils is still used by
many companies for cars of an older vintage.

Most private passenger vehicles are insured under the
family policy. There are two other forms under which this insurance is written—the *basic policy* and the *special policy*.

The exclusions from coverage are few. The insuring clause does not stipulate the hazards that are covered but is drawn to cover any loss or damage with the exception of perils specifically listed.

Basically, the policy excludes loss due to war, damage due to and confined to wear and tear, freezing, mechanical or electrical breakdown or failure, and loss for any automobile used for public or private hire. There is also an exclusion relating to tires unless damaged by fire, malicious mischief, or vandalism, or stolen, unless the loss coincides with other loss covered under the policy. The most important exclusion is loss resulting from collision or upset of the vehicle.

Outside of these exceptions, the policy covers any loss or damage. The coverage is more complete than that of fire or theft policies with all their available supplementary coverages added. Thus, the *comprehensive physical damage policy* will cover fire and lightning, scorching, staining, and spotting, riot and civil commotion, vandalism and malicious mischief, strikes, and almost any damage willfully inflicted on the vehicle. It will insure the car against submersion in water, abnormal tides, rain, sleet, snow, sand storm, and dust storm. Not only theft but damage from attempted theft is covered, with the coverage broadened to include theft by an employee or member of the policyholder's family and virtually every form of embezzlement. All transportation losses are covered, as is damage from missiles or falling objects, whether aircraft or not.

"Actual cash value" or "stated amount"

The comprehensive physical damage policy, as well as the separate fire and theft policies, is usually written in one of two ways. Under one form, no specific amount is given for the value of the insured automobile. The words "actual cash value" are inserted in the policy as the amount of insurance and any loss or damage is adjusted on that basis. Under the second type of policy, a specific dollar amount of insurance is stated.

It is important to understand that a "stated amount" policy will not reimburse you for more than the actual cash value of your car at the time of a loss, regardless of the amount stated

The Automobile Theft Record
(1954-1974)

Year	Passenger Car Registrations	Thefts	Ratio of Cars Stolen/Registered
1954	48,468,418	212,900	1 in 228
1955	52,144,739	223,900	1 in 233
1956	54,210,901	259,800	1 in 209
1957	55,917,897	285,600	1 in 196
1958	56,890,558	291,900	1 in 195
1959	59,453,984	297,900	1 in 200
1960	61,682,304	325,900	1 in 189
1961	63,417,358	333,700	1 in 190
1962	66,108,282	364,300	1 in 181
1963	69,055,428	405,400	1 in 170
1964	71,979,341	470,200	1 in 153
1965	75,240,780	494,100	1 in 152
1966	78,107,900	558,100	1 in 140
1967	80,388,431	656,100	1 in 123
1968	83,595,638	779,300	1 in 107
1969	86,914,823	873,600	1 in 99
1970	89,230,567	923,200	1 in 97
1971	92,741,552	942,900	1 in 98
1972	96,980,314	882,200	1 in 110
1973	101,578,539	925,700	1 in 110
1974	104,857,327	973,800	1 in 108

Sources: Federal Bureau of Investigation, Federal Highway Administration

in the policy. Also, if the amount stated in the policy is less than the actual cash value at the time of the loss, the company is liable only for the amount stated in the policy. If you are given a choice between the two approaches to insuring your automobile, you can select the one with the lower premium.

Collision coverage

Comprehensive physical damage insurance will not cover damage to your car caused by collision with another object, whether moving or stationary, except a bird or an animal.

To insure your automobile against collision losses of almost any kind, you will need to purchase *collision coverage*. This will indemnify you for damages sustained as a result of collision of your car with any moving or stationary object (except a bird or an animal) or from upset of the car. This type of damage is paid whether the collision is your fault or not. The few collision losses not covered by the policy are similar to those under the comprehensive physical damage policy.

Because most automobile damages result from collisions, you may find it advisable to carry protection against this hazard. Almost all collision insurance being issued provides that the policyholder must shoulder some part of each collision loss himself. In some states, it is also possible to buy collision insurance under which the policyholder contributes toward only the first collision loss in any policy year.

The most common method of writing collision insurance which requires some contribution from the insured person is to include a "deductible" figure in the policy. This sum is deducted from the amount the company pays in settlement of each collision loss. Most companies offer a choice of deductibles—$50, $100, $250, and so forth. The company is then liable for only the amount of the damage in any collision which is in excess of this deductible. Thus, if your collision insurance incorporates a deductible of $50 and the damage to your car in a collision totals $125, the company pays $75 toward this loss. The $50 deductible figure will also be deducted from each subsequent claim you present under the policy.

Because small claims are very numerous and also as expensive to administer as larger claims, the reduction in premium is substantial when a higher deductible is incorporated in the policy. Rates also vary with the make of the automobile and the area in which it is principally used.

Do you need collision insurance?

Your individual situation will best determine your need for collision insurance. Most automobile owners can usually meet the smaller collision damages to their cars without undue hardship. To provide some insurance against the heavier damages, collision insurance with a large deductible may be purchased. Under a $250 deductible clause, it is true, you will not be indemnified for the majority of collision losses because many of these losses are less than $250, but with insurance of this kind you will not have to carry the complete burden of heavier damages caused by a more serious collision. Furthermore, the larger deductible may reduce an otherwise prohibitive premium to the point where it is within your means.

Priority should be given to carrying adequate limits under the automobile liability policy. If it becomes necessary, because of the costs involved, to choose between collision insurance and high liability limits, the latter should be given preference. While it is true that the investment in an automobile can be fairly substantial, it may be outweighed many times over by an award for bodily injuries, which, theoretically at least, is virtually without any maximum limit.

Applying for insurance

When applying for automobile insurance, be sure to give an accurate description of the vehicle, the city or town in which it will be principally garaged, your occupation, and whether the car will be used in the regular duties of your work.

If any other company has refused during the past year to issue a policy to you or has canceled or declined to renew insurance on your car, you should inform the insurance company of these facts.

The application will also ask you to furnish the names, ages, and driving records of all members of your household who will drive the vehicle. All these questions and any others put to you by the company should be answered accurately and completely. Remember that misstatement or concealment of

The Boom in Automobile Insurance
Total Premium Payments, 1952-1974

Year	Liability	Collision	Fire, Theft, & Comprehensive
1952	$ 1,917,910,000	$1,087,014,000	$ 425,442,000
1953	2,257,440,000	1,203,498,000	449,805,000
1954	2,366,340,000	1,142,174,000	431,331,000
1955	2,495,020,000	1,239,941,000	487,770,000
1956	2,684,270,000	1,135,122,000	478,172,000
1957	3,003,290,000	1,204,441,000	544,553,000
1958	3,314,660,000	1,180,722,000	593,110,000
1959	3,681,700,000	1,284,980,000	670,217,000
1960	3,882,917,000	1,282,886,000	711,043,000
1961	4,022,762,000	1,251,518,000	712,967,000
1962	4,239,761,000	1,361,378,000	712,752,000
1963	4,526,801,000	1,469,528,000	842,988,000
1964	4,886,444,000	1,602,602,000	905,901,000
1965	5,423,674,000	1,849,073,000	1,011,746,000
1966	6,046,047,000	2,142,143,000	1,115,923,000
1967	6,564,938,000	2,289,172,000	1,168,657,000
1968	7,106,642,000	2,509,105,000	1,257,136,000
1969	7,866,013,000	2,805,146,000	1,391,715,000
1970	8,958,243,000	3,196,584,000	1,626,980,000
1971	9,976,931,000	3,590,748,000	1,848,479,000
1972	10,494,430,000	6,015,860,000*	
1973	10,756,771,000	6,418,990,000	
1974	12,009,634,000	7,059,685,000	

*Since 1972, collision, fire, theft, and comprehensive totals have been combined.

Automobile insurance is the largest classification in the property-liability business. Total premium payments of over $19 billion in 1974 represented about 42 percent of all payments for property-liability insurance.

Sources: *Best's Aggregates & Averages*, Insurance Information Institute

any material fact in your application may void the insurance and leave you stripped of the protection you need at the time of a loss.

When car is not used

If you do not make any use of your car during certain months of the year, you will nevertheless probably want to continue the comprehensive physical damage insurance on the vehicle because it will still be exposed to the risk of loss or damage by fire, theft, windstorm, flood, or other hazard (except perhaps if you put the car into dead storage in an insured facility). The liability insurance and the collision coverage can be suspended by notifying the company when you cease using the car. When you resume operation of the vehicle, you can have the insurance reinstated. A premium rebate will be granted for the period during which insurance was not in effect. Usually, a rebate is not allowed for a suspension which lasts less than sixty days.

Even if you are quite certain that you will be using your automobile for only part of the year, do not have the policy written for the short term. The special table of charges used for such periods results in premiums considerably higher than the proportion of the year involved. Thus, if you asked when insuring your car to have the policy written for six months, you would be charged 70 percent of the full annual premium. Also, do not cancel the policy before its normal expiration date if you are withdrawing the insured automobile from use for a temporary period, for this would incur the short-rate penalty. It would be more advantageous to have the policy written for the full year and suspended during periods when you do not operate the automobile.

If you plan to take your automobile outside of the United States, its territories or possessions, or Canada, be sure to notify the insurance company. Your policy, unless appropriately endorsed, does not cover loss or damage sustained outside these areas.

In case of an accident

If you are involved in an accident, procure immediate medical aid for any injured persons.

Note as many details of the circumstances surrounding the accident as possible, and take the names and addresses of all available witnesses.

Notify the insurance company or its representative immediately of any accident or loss in which your automobile is involved. If theft, larceny, or pilferage take place, notify the police as well as the insurance company.

You should make every effort to protect the car from further damage or loss. Thus, if your automobile is disabled as the result of an accident, try to avoid leaving it where it may be stripped or wrecked. The insurance company will pay for all reasonable expenses you incur to protect the car from further damage.

If a claim is made or a suit is brought against you in connection with an accident, immediately forward to your insurance company every demand, notice, summons, or other process received by you.

In auto insurance, as in all the other types of coverage analyzed in this book, you can reduce your expenses and anxiety by fulfilling the insurance company's requirements so that the policies you have carefully chosen will provide the maximum protection against the perils which face you and your family.

Appendix

Appendix I

Mortality Tables

The American Experience mortality table was published in 1868 as a part of New York law. Covering the years 1843-1858, it was the first mortality table based on experience of insured lives in America and is no longer in use. The Commissioners Standard Ordinary table of mortality published in 1958 was based on experience of insured lives in 1950-1954 and has been used to determine reserves for ordinary life insurance.

Age	American Experience (1843-1858)		Commissioners 1958 Standard Ordinary (1950-1954)		United States Total Population (1969-1971)	
	Deaths per 1,000	Expectation of Life (Years)	Deaths per 1,000	Expectation of Life (Years)	Deaths per 1,000	Expectation of Life (Years)
0	154.70	41.45	7.08	68.30	20.02	70.75
1	63.49	47.94	1.76	67.78	1.25	71.19
2	35.50	50.16	1.52	66.90	.86	70.28
3	23.91	50.98	1.46	66.00	.69	69.34
4	17.70	51.22	1.40	65.10	.57	68.39
5	13.60	51.13	1.35	64.19	.51	67.43
6	11.37	50.83	1.30	63.27	.46	66.46
7	9.75	50.41	1.26	62.35	.43	65.49
8	8.63	49.90	1.23	61.43	.39	64.52
9	7.90	49.33	1.21	60.51	.34	63.54
10	7.49	48.72	1.21	59.58	.31	62.57
11	7.52	48.08	1.23	58.65	.30	61.58
12	7.54	47.45	1.26	57.72	.35	60.60
13	7.57	46.80	1.32	56.80	.46	59.62
14	7.60	46.16	1.39	55.87	.63	58.65
15	7.63	45.50	1.46	54.95	.82	57.69
16	7.66	44.85	1.54	54.03	1.01	56.73
17	7.69	44.19	1.62	53.11	1.17	55.79
18	7.73	43.53	1.69	52.19	1.28	54.86
19	7.77	42.87	1.74	51.28	1.34	53.93
20	7.80	42.20	1.79	50.37	1.40	53.00
21	7.86	41.53	1.83	49.46	1.47	52.07
22	7.91	40.85	1.86	48.55	1.52	51.15
23	7.96	40.17	1.89	47.64	1.53	50.22
24	8.01	39.49	1.91	46.73	1.51	49.30
25	8.06	38.81	1.93	45.82	1.47	48.37

Age	American Experience (1843-1858)		Commissioners 1958 Standard Ordinary (1950-1954)		United States Total Population (1969-1971)	
	Deaths per 1,000	Expectation of Life (Years)	Deaths per 1,000	Expectation of Life (Years)	Deaths per 1,000	Expectation of Life (Years)
26	8.13	38.12	1.96	44.90	1.43	47.44
27	8.20	37.43	1.99	43.99	1.42	46.51
28	8.26	36.73	2.03	43.08	1.44	45.58
29	8.34	36.03	2.08	42.16	1.49	44.64
30	8.43	35.33	2.13	41.25	1.55	43.71
31	8.51	34.63	2.19	40.34	1.63	42.77
32	8.61	33.92	2.25	39.43	1.72	41.84
33	8.72	33.21	2.32	38.51	1.83	40.92
34	8.83	32.50	2.40	37.60	1.95	39.99
35	8.95	31.78	2.51	36.69	2.09	39.07
36	9.09	31.07	2.64	35.78	2.25	38.15
37	9.23	30.35	2.80	34.88	2.44	37.23
38	9.41	29.62	3.01	33.97	2.66	36.32
39	9.59	28.90	3.25	33.07	2.90	35.42
40	9.79	28.18	3.53	32.18	3.14	34.52
41	10.01	27.45	3.84	31.29	3.41	33.63
42	10.25	26.72	4.17	30.41	3.70	32.74
43	10.52	26.00	4.53	29.54	4.04	31.86
44	10.83	25.27	4.92	28.67	4.43	30.99
45	11.16	24.54	5.35	27.81	4.84	30.12
46	11.56	23.81	5.83	26.95	5.28	29.27
47	12.00	23.08	6.36	26.11	5.74	28.42
48	12.51	22.36	6.95	25.27	6.24	27.58
49	13.11	21.63	7.60	24.45	6.78	26.75
50	13.78	20.91	8.32	23.63	7.38	25.93

Mortality Tables

(continued)

Age	American Experience (1843-1858)		Commissioners 1958 Standard Ordinary (1950-1954)		United States Total Population (1969-1971)	
	Deaths per 1,000	Expectation of Life (Years)	Deaths per 1,000	Expectation of Life (Years)	Deaths per 1,000	Expectation of Life (Years)
51	14.54	20.20	9.11	22.82	8.04	25.12
52	15.39	19.49	9.96	22.03	8.76	24.32
53	16.33	18.79	10.89	21.25	9.57	23.53
54	17.40	18.09	11.90	20.47	10.43	22.75
55	18.57	17.40	13.00	19.71	11.36	21.99
56	19.89	16.72	14.21	18.97	12.36	21.23
57	21.34	16.05	15.54	18.23	13.41	20.49
58	22.94	15.39	17.00	17.51	14.52	19.76
59	24.72	14.74	18.59	16.81	15.70	19.05
60	26.69	14.10	20.34	16.12	16.95	18.34
61	28.88	13.47	22.24	15.44	18.29	17.65
62	31.29	12.86	24.31	14.78	19.74	16.97
63	33.94	12.26	26.57	14.14	21.33	16.30
64	36.87	11.67	29.04	13.51	23.06	15.65
65	40.13	11.10	31.75	12.90	24.95	15.00
66	43.71	10.54	34.74	12.31	26.99	14.38
67	47.65	10.00	38.04	11.73	29.18	13.76
68	52.00	9.47	41.68	11.17	31.52	13.16
69	56.76	8.97	45.61	10.64	34.00	12.57
70	61.99	8.48	49.79	10.12	36.61	12.00
71	67.67	8.00	54.15	9.63	39.43	11.43
72	73.73	7.55	58.65	9.15	42.66	10.88
73	80.18⁻	7.11	63.26	8.69	46.44	10.34
74	87.03	6.68	68.12	8.24	50.75	9.82
75	94.37	6.27	73.37	7.81	55.52	9.32
76	102.31	5.88	79.18	7.39	60.60	8.84
77	111.06	5.49	85.70	6.98	65.96	8.38
78	120.83	5.11	93.06	6.59	71.53	7.93
79	131.73	4.74	101.19	6.21	77.41	7.51
80	144.47	4.39	109.98	5.85	83.94	7.10
81	158.60	4.05	119.35	5.51	91.22	6.70

Age	American Experience (1843-1858)		Commissioners 1958 Standard Ordinary (1950-1954)		United States Total Population (1969-1971)	
	Deaths per 1,000	Expectation of Life (Years)	Deaths per 1,000	Expectation of Life (Years)	Deaths per 1,000	Expectation of Life (Years)
82	174.30	3.71	129.17	5.19	98.92	6.32
83	191.56	3.39	139.38	4.89	106.95	5.96
84	211.36	3.08	150.01	4.60	115.48	5.62
85	235.55	2.77	161.14	4.32	125.61	5.28
86	265.68	2.47	172.82	4.06	137.48	4.97
87	303.02	2.18	185.13	3.80	149.79	4.68
88	346.69	1.91	198.25	3.55	161.58	4.42
89	395.86	1.66	212.46	3.31	172.92	4.18
90	454.55	1.42	228.14	3.06	185.02	3.94
91	532.47	1.19	245.77	2.82	198.88	3.73
92	634.26	.98	265.93	2.58	213.63	3.53
93	734.18	.80	289.30	2.33	228.70	3.35
94	857.14	.64	316.66	2.07	243.36	3.19
95	1,000.00	.50	351.24	1.80	257.45	3.06
96			400.56	1.51	269.59	2.95
97			488.42	1.18	280.24	2.85
98			668.15	.83	289.77	2.76
99			1,000.00	.50	298.69	2.69
100					306.96	2.62
101					314.61	2.56
102					321.67	2.51
103					328.17	2.46
104					334.14	2.41
105					339.60	2.37
106					344.60	2.34
107					349.17	2.30
108					353.33	2.27
109					357.12	2.24

Source: Institute of Life Insurance

Appendix II
How Premium Rates Vary

Annual premiums per $1,000 of **1-year renewable** and convertible non-participating term insurance for a man:

Age	Low	High
20	$ 2.22	$ 3.79
25	2.22	3.85
30	2.49	3.90
35	2.81	4.19
40	3.89	5.11
45	5.80	6.99
50	9.08	10.03
55	13.51	15.15
60	19.73	23.37
64	28.29	33.06

Annual premiums per $1,000 of **5-year renewable** and convertible non-participating term insurance for a man:

Age	Low	High
20	$ 2.10	$ 4.66
25	2.21	4.89
30	2.45	5.12
35	3.09	6.14
40	4.25	8.18
45	6.62	10.62
50	9.94	14.59
55	15.00	20.30
60	24.53	30.47
64	36.97	39.06

Annual premiums per $1,000 of **straight-life** cash-value nonparticipating insurance for a man:

Age	Low	High
20	$10.54	$12.09
25	12.15	14.03
30	14.18	16.45
35	17.04	19.46
40	20.79	23.38
45	25.34	28.78
50	31.27	36.07
55	39.75	44.28
60	51.14	54.94
65	66.47	72.46

Note: The premium rate usually decreases if a large amount of insurance is purchased. In addition to the premium, most companies charge an annual policy fee ranging from about $10 to $20.

Appendix III

Health Insurance Benefits by State

State	Paid by Insurance Companies (in millions), 1973	Paid by Blue Cross, Blue Shield, and Other Hospital-Medical Plans (in millions), 1973
Alabama	$ 169	$ 138
Alaska	12	5
Arizona	134	56
Arkansas	83	55
California	1,477	1,084
Colorado	121	129
Connecticut	200	218
Delaware	23	54
District of Columbia	87	223
Florida	461	182
Georgia	344	107
Hawaii	14	76
Idaho	35	22
Illinois	868	504
Indiana	356	265
Iowa	149	130
Kansas	101	127
Kentucky	132	135
Louisiana	195	84
Maine	42	44
Maryland	164	209
Massachusetts	277	495
Michigan	582	999
Minnesota	241	123
Mississippi	99	52
Missouri	330	257
Montana	36	23

State	Paid by Insurance Companies (in millions), 1973	Paid by Blue Cross, Blue Shield, and Other Hospital-Medical Plans (in millions), 1973
Nebraska	$ 85	$ 56
Nevada	46	5
New Hampshire	27	42
New Jersey	330	445
New Mexico	53	18
New York	877	1,600
North Carolina	265	157
North Dakota	22	34
Ohio	628	787
Oklahoma	149	71
Oregon	110	134
Pennsylvania	522	891
Rhode Island	20	93
South Carolina	135	65
South Dakota	35	11
Tennessee	244	152
Texas	750	443
Utah	47	46
Vermont	17	27
Virginia	224	174
Washington	164	209
West Virginia	89	111
Wisconsin	277	287
Wyoming	15	13
Total U.S.	$11,863	$11,667

Note: Benefits shown for "Insurance Companies" include loss-of-income payments.

Health Insurance Benefits by State

(continued)

State	Average Cost per Hospital Stay, 1973	Average Length Hospital Stay In Days, 1973	Average Hospital Cost per Day, 1973
Alabama	$ 649.05	7.5	$ 86.54
Alaska	806.30	4.8	167.98
Arizona	969.34	7.2	134.63
Arkansas	515.16	6.7	76.89
California	923.27	6.6	139.89
Colorado	736.03	6.6	111.52
Connecticut	1,129.51	7.6	148.62
Delaware	1,036.56	8.2	126.41
District of Columbia	1,271.33	8.2	155.04
Florida	806.40	7.5	107.52
Georgia	669.26	6.7	99.89
Hawaii	873.01	7.3	119.59
Idaho	607.92	6.8	89.40
Illinois	994.01	8.3	119.76
Indiana	770.48	7.9	97.53
Iowa	662.14	7.8	84.89
Kansas	688.97	7.8	88.33
Kentucky	615.85	7.1	86.74
Louisiana	647.99	6.6	98.18
Maine	742.66	7.4	100.36
Maryland	1,163.74	8.3	140.21
Massachusetts	1,320.79	8.6	153.58
Michigan	1,054.68	8.3	127.07
Minnesota	831.95	8.8	94.54
Mississippi	527.38	7.0	75.34
Missouri	805.48	8.4	95.89
Montana	561.13	6.6	85.02

State	Average Cost per Hospital Stay, 1973	Average Length Hospital Stay In Days, 1973	Average Hospital Cost per Day, 1973
Nebraska	$ 722.82	8.4	$ 86.05
Nevada	855.37	6.8	125.79
New Hampshire	682.27	7.2	94.76
New Jersey	982.08	8.8	111.60
New Mexico	639.27	5.9	108.35
New York	1,430.11	9.8	145.93
North Carolina	664.09	7.6	87.38
North Dakota	629.97	8.3	75.90
Ohio	884.62	8.2	107.88
Oklahoma	637.30	6.8	93.72
Oregon	742.46	6.4	116.01
Pennsylvania	963.07	8.9	108.21
Rhode Island	1,171.22	8.5	137.79
South Carolina	589.39	7.2	81.86
South Dakota	546.77	7.3	74.90
Tennessee	672.68	7.6	88.51
Texas	680.40	7.0	97.20
Utah	663.93	5.8	114.47
Vermont	807.65	8.1	99.71
Virginia	753.33	8.2	91.87
Washington	741.51	5.7	130.09
West Virginia	629.48	7.7	81.75
Wisconsin	820.93	8.4	97.73
Wyoming	482.28	6.0	80.38
Total U.S.	$ 893.57	7.8	$114.56

Sources: Health Insurance Institute, American Hospital Association, Health Insurance Association of America

Appendix IV

The Catastrophe Record
(1969-1974)

Catastrophes resulting in insured losses of over $10 million are listed.

Date	Place	Catastrophe	Estimated Loss Payments
1969			
Jan.-Dec.	Many localities	Disorders	$ 31,300,000
June 17-18	Amarillo and Texas Panhandle, western Oklahoma, central Texas	Wind, hail	20,000,000
Aug. 17-18	Louisiana, Mississippi, Alabama, Florida	Hurricane "Camille"	165,300,000*
1970			
May 11-12	Texas Panhandle (Lubbock)	Tornado, wind, hail	50,000,000
Aug. 3	Southeastern Texas	Hurricane "Celia"	309,950,000
Sept. 22-25	Oakland-Berkeley Hills and southern California	Fires	24,848,000
1971			
Feb. 9	Los Angeles County	Earthquake, fire	31,600,000
Feb. 21-22	Texas, Louisiana, Tennessee, Georgia, Mississippi, Alabama, Indiana, Ohio, North Carolina	Tornadoes, wind	12,700,000
Apr. 22-23	Oklahoma, Texas, Arkansas, Mississippi, Alabama, Tennessee	Wind, hail, tornado	12,000,000
May 5-10	Texas, Oklahoma, Missouri, Iowa, Kansas, Illinois, Louisiana, Arkansas, Tennessee	Wind, hail, tornado	13,000,000
Aug. 27-28	Atlantic coastal states	Tropical storm "Doria"	13,500,000
1972			
Jan. 25	Maine, New Hampshire, Vermont, Massachusetts, Rhode Island, Connecticut, New York, New Jersey, Pennsylvania	Windstorm	11,050,000

Date	Place	Catastrophe	Estimated Loss Payments
1972			
Apr. 30	Kansas and Oklahoma	Wind, hail, tornado	$13,770,000
June 9-10	South Dakota	Flood	12,520,000
June 17-25	Florida, Georgia, South Carolina, North Carolina, Virginia, West Virginia, Ohio, Michigan, Maine, Pennsylvania, Maryland, Delaware, D.C., New Jersey, New York, Connecticut, Rhode Island, Massachusetts, Vermont	Hurricane "Agnes"	97,853,000**
1973			
Mar. 31-Apr. 1	Georgia, South Carolina, Virginia	Wind, hail, tornadoes	33,352,000
Apr. 19-26	North Dakota, South Dakota, Minnesota, New Mexico, Texas, Oklahoma, Arkansas, Alabama, Missouri, Illinois, Iowa, Louisiana, Mississippi, Florida, Georgia	Wind, hail, tornadoes	33,105,000
May 10-11	Arkansas, Tennesse, Missouri, Kentucky, Indiana, Ohio, Illinois, Kansas, Oklahoma, Alabama, South Carolina	Wind, hail, tornadoes	21,934,000
May 26-29	Alabama, Arkansas, Florida, Georgia, Illinois, Indiana, Kansas, Kentucky, Louisiana, Mississippi, Missouri, New Jersey, North Carolina, Ohio, Oklahoma, Pennsylvania, South Carolina, Tennessee, Texas, Virginia, West Virginia	Wind, hail, tornadoes	76,490,000
June 29-30, July 1	New Hampshire, Vermont, New York, Pennsylvania, Texas	Wind, hail, tornadoes, flood	10,685,000

The Catastrophe Record

(continued)

Date	Place	Catastrophe	Estimated Loss Payments
1974			
Mar. 20-21	Alabama, Georgia, Louisiana, Mississippi	Wind, hail, tornadoes	$ 15,028,000
Apr. 1-2	Alabama, Kentucky, Tennessee, Ohio	Wind, hail, tornadoes	11,700,000
Apr. 2-5	Alabama, Arkansas, Georgia, Illinois, Indiana, Kentucky, Michigan, Mississippi, Ohio, Missouri, North Carolina, Oklahoma, South Carolina, Tennessee, Texas, Virginia, West Virginia	Wind, hail, tornadoes	430,566,000
Apr. 13-15	Michigan, Ohio, Tennessee, Texas, West Virginia	Wind, hail, tornadoes	11,990,000
May 22-26	Kansas, Oklahoma, Texas	Wind, hail,	23,640,000
June 6-7	Arkansas, Oklahoma	Wind, hail, tornadoes	12,755,000
June 8-9	Kansas, Oklahoma	Wind, hail, tornadoes	47,512,400
June 18-21	Illinois, Indiana, Iowa, Minnesota, Wisconsin	Wind, hail, tornadoes	20,191,000
Sept. 7-8	Louisiana	Hurricane "Carmen"	14,721,000
Nov. 30-Dec. 2	Delaware, Maryland, Ohio, Virginia, Pennsylvania, New Jersey, New York, Michigan	Wind, snow, flood	16,773,000

* Includes fixed property losses only. Total insured loss from "Camille" estimated at $225 million.

** "Agnes" caused extensive uninsured losses, largely as a result of flooding. Total property damage estimated at $3,097,800,000.

Sources: American Insurance Association, Insurance Services Office, Insurance Information Institute, National Oceanic and Atmospheric Administration

Index